STOLEN CHILDREN

STOLEN CHILDREN

How and Why Parents Kidnap Their Kids— And What to Do about It

John Edward Gill

SEAVIEW BOOKS

NEW YORK

To *Alison*, who endures

MANUFACTURED IN THE UNITED STATES OF AMERICA.

FIRST EDITION

Library of Congress Cataloging in Publication Data

Gill, John Edward.
   Stolen children.

     1. Kidnapping, Parental—United States. 2. Custody of children—United States. I. Title.
HV6598.G54   362.8′2   80–52404
ISBN 0–87223–667–6

Designed by M. Franklin-Plympton

Contents

Acknowledgments

I would like to thank the following people for their help and cooperation in gathering material for this book: Liz McNichols, research assistant to Senator Charles Mathias, Bob Hirschfeld, Nat Denman, Betsy Warrior, Sarah Keegan, Lois Jenks, Rod Bivings, Joanne Johnson, Charles Van Duzee, Stephen Lee, Carol Zimmerman, Gabriel Kohn, Joe Brandine, Robert Brink, Vert Vergon, Ken Lewis, Bill Burke, Dr. Daniel O'Leary, Grace Rienhoff, and Pat Hoff.

There were many people whose patience and understanding made this book possible. In particular I'd like to thank Russell Galen, Anne Harrison, and Dr. Lawrence J. Epstein.

John Gill
Stony Brook, N.Y.
April 1981

Author's Note

In order to accurately and completely discuss the problem of child stealing, it has been necessary to include information about behavior that may be criminal in nature. The author does not advocate the breaking of any laws or the committing of any crimes. Such information is merely presented as part of an overall effort to describe the problem in its entirety.

In order to protect privacy, names of parents have been changed.

J.G.

And I think that saving a little child
and fotching him to his own,
Is a derned sight better business
Than loafing around the Throne.

—John Milton Hay (1838–1905)
"Jim Bludso"

STOLEN CHILDREN

1

One Woman's Story

Pamela Smith was a thirty-four-year-old housewife who lived in Paramus, New Jersey, with her husband, Stan, and their three children—Sean, ten, Megan, eight, and Heather, six. Pam spent two years in the Peace Corps before marrying her husband, a pilot with an international airline. They were married ten years.

On Tuesday morning, May 31, 1977, she went to a divorce lawyer. She and Stan had problems. He was away most of the time; they couldn't agree on discipline for their children, monthly budgets for their family, even how they might separate.

"We discussed divorce several times," she said, "and what he wanted us to do was get an apartment, something equal to our home, and we would share it. He was gone about half the time. He wanted me to clear out and go to the apartment whenever he came home. But there was no way I would do that."

One day, while at a friend's house to write her complaint, she felt strange. "I called at noon and there was no answer," she said. Her children usually came home for lunch. When she came home at 12:30 P.M., the house was empty. There was no furniture, no refrigerator, even. Just her clothes.

Her husband had typed a note and left it on a wall: "Pam, the kids and I have gone on a big vacation."

She called the police from a neighbor's house. They told her there was no law to stop a father from vacationing with his children. Her lawyer agreed. "I had never served papers on my husband and until I did there was no way of doing anything legal. This was frustrating," she said.

For the next few months Pam Smith lived with neighbors and friends, borrowing money. Stan had the electricity and phone service cut off, but did make payments on their brown ranch-style home. She called his friends and went to the airline, but didn't get much help at first.

"In August, I found out through another pilot that Stan was due back at Kennedy Airport one night," she said. "So I put on a wig, sunglasses, and someone else's clothes, and hired an investigator in New York and met his plane. We had papers that gave me temporary custody, told him to turn over the children, and to appear in court.

"I didn't recognize him at first," she said. "He had lost so much weight. He had grown a moustache, his hair was longer. He just looked like a whole different person."

Stan never showed up in court for the divorce trial and didn't return the children. "My lawyer thought he'd been to Florida and was trying to establish residency," she said. "That way we'd have to go into court there, under Florida law. I knew if we did, I'd have a terrible fight."

There was nothing she could do but think about her children, wonder where to turn, try to get through each day and night. "When it first happened I was in total shock," she said. "I couldn't eat. I couldn't sleep. People talk about heart-aches. Well, my heart was broken. It ached physically. I felt at first the only thing I could do was pray."

She turned to friends, but "the people I thought would help me most couldn't take it. My very best friend didn't speak. She said I was looking too good and acting too happy. She said, 'You're not carrying this right and you're dumping it all over others.'

"I was doing what I could, trying to cope. I knew if I was a sad sack, crying all the time and a total wreck, I would alienate people. I mean, people can't carry stuff like this, particularly where children are involved, and especially when they're good friends of yours and have children of their own. It broke people's hearts, but they didn't know what to say. They would just start crying on the phone and hang up.

"One girl said, 'How can you carry on?' But there were others who admired me. They said that even though it was so bad, it wasn't hard to be around me because I didn't carry a terrible burden.

"I don't know how I did it, but I felt strong all the time, and knew what I had to do—find my children—and I prayed. It sounds crazy, but you do whatever you have to. I just put it out of my hands and surrendered and said, 'Hey, you know this is all I've been doing for some months.' I really learned to live one day at a time.

"In the beginning I couldn't eat so I made these eggnog concoctions. I would throw those down and jog and run my feet off, run until I dropped."

She began sending registered letters to her children through a post office box Stan had at La Guardia Airport. But there were no replies.

Pamela Smith, suburban housewife turned amateur private investigator, learned her husband was in Jacksonville, Florida, because her lawyer subpoenaed his airline for his address. But she didn't know *where* in Jacksonville because the address his airline gave was false. She'd hoped Stan would have school records sent down. But when school started in September, there was no request.

Her luck soon turned. Stan called a friend to say that he was still in Jacksonville, only at a different address. Rumor had it he was moving soon to Los Angeles. A friend of Pam's, a school principal in New Jersey, called school districts in Jacksonville and learned where the children were in class. Most important, he found where they lived. It was now the end of September.

"I hired an investigator right out of the Yellow Pages," she said, "which my lawyer had told me to do. I explained the situation briefly and they said, 'Fine, we have cases like this all the time, wire us two hundred dollars.' They wanted another five hundred and I told them to watch the house, to see if my children really *were* there. But I never heard from them again. I spent a hundred and twelve dollars in October calling back and forth to Florida to track them down, but I couldn't reach them again."

Stan tried to throw her off. A little girl down the street in Paramus got a letter from Megan postmarked Miami. Someone else got a card from Fort Lauderdale. But toward the end of October a pilot from his airline told her Stan would leave Florida soon. It would be a three-day flight and he would take off Sunday, October 30.

"Against everyone's advice, I made plans to go," Pam said. "I wrestled with myself so long over whether to get them [her children]. I'd had an answering service put in the home, thinking they would call. They were old enough and I was concerned as to why they didn't. I thought maybe they didn't want to, or maybe Stan had turned them against me. Maybe they *were* happier where they were, and I prepared myself for the fact they might not want to come home.

"So I spent a long time figuring that out, but then decided that even if I couldn't get them or even if they didn't want me, I could at least tell them I loved them and had been trying to reach them.

"I had it all figured out, that even if I couldn't physically bring them home it was going to work, no matter what. The trip, at least, my flying down and searching."

With a friend, Don Birns, she flew down on Saturday night, October 29, and drove around Stan's neighborhood, looking for a place to park and watch the house. All the draperies were pulled and it didn't look like there were children around.

"There were a lot of houses for sale," she said, "and we thought of going in and saying we were interested in buying there and finding out what the schools were like; if there were any parks in the area and where they might be. That sort of thing.

"But we decided that wouldn't work. It was Sunday now and we had found a good parking spot the night before, so we just drove over the next morning around eleven and parked about half a block from the house and waited. I guess we waited for about an hour or so.

"I was very nervous. I hadn't seen my children for five months. Around noon Don said, 'Let's get some lunch,' but I had a funny feeling, call it luck, if you like, and said people do things at noon sometimes."

The children came out at ten minutes after twelve.

"My little boy rode his bicycle. It was a clear day, warm, and I thought suddenly it had gotten cloudy, but then I realized my face was wet. I told myself this wasn't the time to be emotional and I fought to control myself, fought hard. I'd worn a wig and dark glasses the night before, but now I didn't have them and I guess it was just as well because I might have scared him.

"I panicked and didn't know what to do. I'd called the police and district attorney in New Jersey when Stan had first taken them, the FBI in Manhattan, too, and they hadn't done anything. They said my husband hadn't broken any laws. Now I wondered if the police in Florida would do anything to stop *me*.

"Don, my friend, said just wait, and then Megan, my daughter, came out on her bicycle. The children went in different directions, with Megan riding toward us. We just drove slowly forward and stopped at her side, and I had trouble seeing again. It was so emotional. There was my daughter just a few feet away, and it had been a long five months.

"It was really good that I had somebody with me because I couldn't have handled it myself. Don had the sense to get out with me and take her bike and put it in the back of the station wagon we'd rented so it wouldn't look like somebody had taken her.

"I asked if she wanted to come with me—I knew that I was going to do that, to ask her. I didn't want to grab any of them. Megan, she just stood with her mouth open and was in shock. She said, 'Mommy,' and I hadn't heard that word in so long. I held her and asked again if she wanted to come with me. Yet I was in a hurry, so I jumped back in the car with her and we hugged, and I forgot for a moment about the time. Megan and I shook and cried, and then I knew Heather was the only one who hadn't come out of the house and I knew we couldn't leave because she was the youngest.

"I asked if Heather would come out and Megan said No, because she had on her Halloween costume and Mrs. Klaus, the woman my husband had hired as a housekeeper, wouldn't let her out.

"Megan said she'd go inside and tell her [Heather] someone was outside to see her. I said, 'Yes, you've got to do this and it has to be done right and if you have to wait for her, do it, do it. You have to get her out now and we're not going home without her.'

"So, she went back in the house and I thought, My children are gone again."

Don Birns said that Sean was still outside. "That gave us something to do while Megan and Heather were inside with the housekeeper," Pam said. "As we started to drive to where we'd seen my son leave his bike, we saw Megan come out again. She ran after us and said Heather still wasn't allowed out, so we told her to get Sean first.

"Again, we didn't park in front of the house; Megan was with us and I wasn't thinking, but, thank God, she was, and she said, 'I'll tell him the same as I told Heather.' She went up to the house of Sean's friend, and I saw Sean's bike and kept wondering, Maybe one child out of three was better than none at all. But we were here, Don and I, by ourselves, without any help—even private investigators hadn't helped

—and we'd better try to get them all ourselves. It might be our only chance. We really *were* on our own, and here was Megan doing all the work.

"She went up to the house and told Sean through the screen door that she had a surprise for him, but he said he didn't care, he wouldn't come out.

"I could hear him saying that, but he finally did come out on the porch and we just drove up and I rolled down the window and said, 'Sean, Sean,' and he took one look and was furious.

" 'Where have you been? Where have you been?' he kept saying. For a minute I didn't think he was going to come. So I said, 'Sean, I'm here now and I didn't know where you were and I love you,' and he ran and threw his arms around me and cried and jumped into the car.

"Then Megan went and got Heather out of the house by telling her a little friend was waiting. This was a real scene because we backed up and were, again, half a block away when Megan came running out with Heather following in a ghost costume with a gray mask, and I hoped it was her because I couldn't see her face.

"This old woman came after her. She was white-faced and breathing hard and wore a green kimono, like she hadn't expected to go out. But Don backed up the car, going *away* from the house, and the woman didn't see us. She stopped about two houses away, out of breath and tired, looked around and went back inside. Another stroke of luck.

"I got out and picked up Heather, and took off her mask and hugged her. She was crying and I held her, and we drove all day and night, heading for Georgia."

Pamela Smith talked with her children as Don drove.

"The kids were so happy to be with me, and Sean was angry at his father," she said. "He asked why I wasn't saying bad things about Daddy. 'He hated you,' he said. I didn't want to talk badly about their father in front of them. I had photostated all the letters I'd mailed to La Guardia while they were gone. I'd sent them registered and Stan had signed for them and I read them now. We had the children's birth certificates just in case the police stopped us on the way to Savannah. It was one hundred and fifty miles and I couldn't relax at all.

"Their father had lied to them and had told them I had never written. They were angry at him. In Georgia we left their bikes in the rented car and just got on a plane. Before we took off, though, I called Jacksonville and told the house-keeper the children were with me and everything was all right."

But it wasn't all right. Pam's children were scared when they came back to Paramus.

"When we got home, we were all afraid Stan would come and whip them away again," Pam said. "I was in real fear of what he might do. We stayed across from our old house. The children were very frightened to be alone. I couldn't even cross the street without them following me. In fact, during the first few weeks at home they would cry if they had to leave my side.

"I was supposed to go to New York three days after I got them back, and Sean, the ten-year-old, was just devastated. He said, 'You can't leave me. I'm afraid I'm going to lose you. I won't ever see you again.'

"I really had a time with the children, especially when we were brave enough to sleep in our own house," Pam said. "I had no furniture, of course, no beds, no washing machine, nothing. People lent me cots and I slept in the middle of the two little girls, one on each side. I couldn't put them in their own rooms because they wouldn't leave me.

"One night I was putting my little boy to bed and he said he had a fear it would happen again. It bothers me because he's just not happy anymore. He's a loner now and didn't use to be like that. When I ask what's bothering him, I get the same answer: 'Something bad is going to happen.' "

Pamela Smith learned that her children wanted to protect

themselves, even if it meant hiding from the rest of the family. "Every time they would go to the bathroom, they would lock the door," she said. "Whenever they went into a bedroom they would lock the door. They were locking themselves in any room they went into. If two of us would go into a room together, they would *still* lock the door.

"Also, they go off and cry more easily now than they used to. They are more delicate. They're not resilient, they don't bounce back if they've had a scolding. I don't go out without them, even for a while on weekends, for instance. It's not like I can get a sitter or a friend to come in, and go out shopping for three hours on Saturday afternoon."

After several months her children were not quite as frightened. Pam also had gained some perspective on their abduction and had allowed Stan to see them.

"I've been dealing with him," she said. "I sat down and wrote him a letter, and we're trying to work things out out of court. He's going to be difficult, but the one thing I really want to do is tell him if he doesn't send support, he can't see his children. But I don't want to do that, actually. It would only hurt them.

"He says I've turned them against him, which is absolutely the opposite. If anything, I've spent many hours trying to explain why Daddy acts like he does and that he is really not a bad person, but he is very angry and sometimes people do bad things. He's thirty-nine, but immature. After ten years of marriage, to walk out like that. I don't know what led him to it. It took a lot of cunning. He planned it for a year or so, one of his friends now tells me."

From her children and some of Stan's friends, she pieced together what had happened in May. "Stan had been listening to my phone conversations from a hookup in the basement," she said. "He knew when I was leaving and must have picked up the children when they came home for lunch. He had a U-Haul van ready to take the furniture. He and a friend took them in his car with the U-Haul hooked in back, and I guess he forgot some of his Air Force stuff (he was a pilot in the reserves) and came back for it. Stan's friend, who was driving the car, said police came up and said something to him and my little boy asked, 'Do you know where my mother is?' But the police never heard him and the kids didn't know what was going on.

"Stan went down to Philadelphia, Pennsylvania, where there's a reserve air station. He's a major in the reserves and they tried to talk him out of leaving with the children, I learned, but he wouldn't be swayed. He drove south the next day, stopping in motels and telling the children I would be coming, and then I never came.

"Evidently he'd had the whole thing set up, because right away he moved into a beautiful home. But why in Jacksonville, I couldn't tell. First of all, it's not near an airport. But I found out from the children that he knew the woman who rented him the house. They said they thought Daddy knew her from before, and he got time off from the airline because he told them all these stories about having nobody to take care of them. He made it look like I'd deserted them.

"He had spread that story around. One pilot who was sympathetic to me at first changed his whole attitude after he'd been on a flight and had talked with Stan. Another pilot said, 'I don't know who to believe. I had no idea you were a sick mother. I'm not allowed to tell you anything.' I got furious with him, saying, 'Who is sick enough to hide children and not let them talk to their mother?'"

Pamela Smith now works as a secretary with a large corporation. Like most parents who have lost children this way, she has tried to figure why Stan did it, why her marriage broke up so suddenly.

"I thought all along that Stan loved them," she said. "It's a strange kind of love, though, to be taking children off like that, with no chance to pack or to say good-bye. He was punishing me, and I have this tremendous guilt, thinking I was a terrible wife and so on, who drove him to it. I graduated from college and had been all over the world before I met him, and I thought I knew what I was doing when I married him.

"He seems stable in the sense of his job. I've learned a lot more about pilots during this. Other pilots tell me it's a certain breed of 'cat' who is an airline pilot. I've seriously wondered how they could keep this man working, because he was obviously under tremendous pressure, with taking the children and worrying that he was going to be tracked down by me with papers every time he touched down.

"His background is quite different from mine. Everybody in his family had been married and divorced at least twice. His father had just died in this kind of a snap, very quickly, from a heart attack. He wasn't the same after that. Nobody knows him, and we've been married so long. I don't know what he wants out of life. I could never sit down and talk with him."

Pam felt the trip south permanently damaged the children's relationship with their father. "They are afraid of him now," she said. "He has a violent temper and they've seen him lose it. When Stan calls, they're not honest with him. They don't tell him anything, and when they hang up they say I want such and such—a present or something on a holiday—and I say, 'Why didn't you tell that to Daddy?' They say they are afraid to. They don't want to go down there and visit him, which he wants them to do. He can see them up here, in the house. I've agreed to that. They should see their father."

Though Pam allows Stan visitation, it is carefully regulated. "He hasn't taken them out of the house yet," she said. "The first time I met with him was with a friend of mine and a friend of his. I had written and said I wanted to meet. He was crazy. The second time I met with him and his lawyer, because I'd told him, 'Do yourself a favor and get a lawyer.' He met his lawyer, but hasn't submitted to New Jersey law. We're still not back in court, although I have temporary custody. We've sat down with our lawyers for hours and hours. He wants the children to spend time this summer with him. This is not going to be the case. I'm not going to sign anything. I haven't gotten any money or heard from him since Christmas, when he said, 'Oh, you haven't gotten any money?' It's like he's playing games. I gave in too much already, letting him speak with the children on the phone and even seeing them in my house."

Pam has no regrets about retrieving her children herself. She is still surprised that her husband didn't legally commit a crime. "When I went to Florida," she said, "I called police there and told them I was coming to snatch my children back. I am their mother. If I have to break in or whatever, I'm going to do it, whether it's against the law or not."

2

An Overview

Pamela Smith is not the only parent to lose children this way.

The government says that child stealing, where a parent involved in a divorce or separation hides with the children, happens about 25,000 times a year. Private groups feel it can happen as many as 100,000 times a year. If you include children who are not returned after a visit to the noncustodial parent, the figure may be as high as 400,000 cases annually, according to Michael Agopian, a Los Angeles criminologist.

No one knows for sure. Police in some states don't keep records of child stealing. In New York, for instance, it is a misdemeanor to interfere with a custody order. But if a parent goes to a precinct with a complaint, it is filed under domestic affairs. Also, many parents don't report it when their children haven't returned from a weekend with the other parent.

In cases where there isn't a custody order there is absolutely no legal complaint to report. A still-married parent has every right to take his or her children wherever and whenever he or she pleases. Parents can lie and say their children have been taken by a stranger. But once police or the FBI learn that the "stranger" is a natural parent or relative, they stop investigating. Local police may stay on if, as in California, violating a custody order is a felony. But rarely will they do more than process necessary paperwork.

Many stolen children are never found. Doris Jonas Freed, chairperson of the committee on custody of the American Bar Association, estimates that six or seven children out of every ten who are stolen are never returned. Senator Alan Cranston of California, cosponsor of a federal bill to help stop the problem, says only 10 percent of the children stolen are ever recovered. And the problem grows, with over a million divorces each year. The Census Bureau estimates that within ten years one-third of all children in America will come from divorced homes.

And with divorce rates soaring, child stealing will become even more commonplace. "The problem of child snatching is greater today than ever before," says Senator Charles Mathias of Maryland. "More than ten million children under the age of eighteen live in families headed by a single parent. With the escalating divorce rate and our increasingly mobile society, these figures are on the rise. The American family and American society are in flux. We are in a whole new ball game where old rules no longer apply; new rules haven't been written. Small wonder that custody disputes have been called potential interstate nightmares."

In 1960 there were 2.2 divorces per 100,000 population; in 1978 there were 5.1 divorces per 100,000 population. As these figures grow, so the number of children involved in divorce has grown, too—from 463,000 in 1960 to 1,117,000 today. And more and more of these divorced parents remain single. In 1960, 8.5 percent of the families in America were single-parent homes—7.4 percent headed by mothers, 1.1 percent headed by fathers. In 1978, 19 percent of all families with children had only one parent living with them. Mothers headed 17 percent of these single-parent families and fathers headed 2 percent. In actual numbers, this means there are almost ten million single-parent families, eight million headed by women, two million headed by men. And with mobility, rising divorce rates, and the lack of federal laws, the frequency of child stealing will increase.

Children who are stolen often become pawns, bartered goods like stocks or real estate, with which to forge a better "deal"—financially, emotionally, legally—in the divorce process. Or they may be kept hidden, ultimate prizes hoarded by a spiteful ex-spouse.

Yet no one breaks a federal law in taking these children. The Lindbergh Law (Title 18 of the United States Code) makes kidnapping a federal crime, but it excludes parents who take and conceal their own children. Local laws differ from state to state. About thirty states, including California and Illinois, treat child stealing as a felony, which means an abductor can be arrested in another state and sent home. Felonies carry a year or more in jail as punishment. But other states, like New York and Pennsylvania, treat concealing children as a minor offense, a misdemeanor, which can carry up to a year's penalty. However, an abducting parent who leaves those states will not be tracked down, either by the FBI or the state police in the state they've moved to.

Under the Uniform Child Custody Jurisdiction Act, states are required to honor a custody order from another state. This new federal law went into effect early in 1981. Approximately forty-three states had already adopted this law voluntarily before then. Only seven states—Massachusetts, Mississippi, New Mexico, Oklahoma, South Carolina, Texas and West Virginia, plus the District of Columbia and Puerto Rico—had not adopted it by the end of 1980.

Drawn up in 1968 by the National Conference of Commissioners on Uniform State Laws, headquartered in Chicago, the act was supposed to prevent parents who lost custody in one state from stealing children and taking them to another state, hoping to get custody there. But even though those forty-three states had adopted it in theory, they ignored it in practice.

And the Act itself is weak. It includes four loopholes that make it quite easy for a new state to take jurisdiction, even if there is a custody order in another state: if the child has lived in the new state for six months; if one parent has a "significant connection" with the new state (i.e., a business or second residence); if there is a threat of child abuse; or if it is in the best interests of the child.

Furthermore, UCCJA will only work if there is a custody order. Most parents steal children *before* going to court. And finally, there is no provision to help one state determine if custody has already been awarded in another state. Chances are that an absconding parent will go into court in a new state without letting the victimized parent or the home state courts know about it.

A further complication arises for parents who have custody of a child in a state that treats child snatching as a misdemeanor, like New Jersey or Delaware. If the child is stolen and taken to a state that treats child snatching as a felony, like Massachusetts or Oklahoma but doesn't recognize custody orders from other states, and the abducting parent wins custody in the second state, the original custodial parent can be accused of committing a felony if he or she tries to recover the child.

This state-by-state handling of child stealing is chaotic, costly, and dangerous. A Michigan mother with custody of her two young daughters found them in Utah, and spent $15,000 on attorneys and private investigators only to have a judge in Salt Lake City award custody to her former husband.

A custodial father in California lost his son to his former wife when she went to Montana and stayed with relatives. Montana gave custody to her relatives because they lived there.

Cases like these push parents into the gray, quasi-legal world of self-help. Some hire professional "custody vigilantes." These men aren't licensed private investigators, but self-proclaimed "civil rights workers" who travel the country looking for stolen children. There are no laws against stealing children for profit, or recovering children for profit, either, as long as a natural parent hires one of these men and goes with them. No laws govern these vigilantes, and they usually cross state lines before police know about them or learn what they've done.

Some parents have taken to the road in station wagons and vans, living from suitcases, camping out in the search for their children. They become migrants, abandoning jobs and homes, working part-time or living on credit. Searching. One father from Long Island, for instance, spent a year searching five western states for his four-year-old daughter. He sold his home and worked part-time to pay for his trip.

Many of these parents believe that because there are no laws to aid them or to prevent abduction by fathers and mothers, they must take the law into their own hands— sometimes even breaking it—to find their sons and daughters. They enter homes, steal address books, open mail, tap phones, forge letters to banks and credit companies, anything to find their ex-husbands and ex-wives. It is the only kind of help they will get.

Yet parents taking the law into their own hands can have tragic consequences. A New Mexico father and his son died in an auto accident after a chase in Oklahoma. A Florida mother was shot to death while trying to stop her ex-husband from stealing their daughter. Other parents have been beaten, sprayed with Mace, or tied up while a former husband or wife, with the aid of friends or vigilantes, has taken children.

Most child thefts are not as dramatic. Parents steal their children from school bus stops, playgrounds, shopping centers. Many just don't return them after a legitimate visit, or move before the other parent *tries* to visit.

Abducting parents move more quickly than married parents. They switch jobs or careers more easily. Some have relatives and friends who help hide them, create alibis, and give false information to the parent who has lost children and who now has become a nuisance, an angry, upset former in-law who calls long distance, pleading or scolding, trying to find where the children are.

The overall effect on parents can be devastating. Many lose weight, quit jobs, waste money on lawyers and private investigators, go on welfare. They have no place to turn. There are only two groups in the country that counsel parents looking for their abducted children. One is in Los Angeles, one is in New York.* But volunteers run them, and they are overrun with parents calling every day, asking what to do.

The government doesn't help. Various agencies that might assist parents of stolen children have resisted requests to find children. The Federal Parent Locator Service will track parents who violate a custody order. Yet most parents steal children *before* custody has been decided. Also, the Parent Locator Service can only find abducting parents who work on the books, paying social security taxes and federal and state income taxes. Most child stealers live underground, work off the books, get paid in cash, and don't pay taxes. The government can't find their salaries or wages listed with any employer or agency. The Parent Locator Service is a civil agency, therefore it can't arrest abducting parents and return stolen children if it finds them.

Parents without custody or visitation must go before a county civil court and ask for an order directing the state parent locator to find their children. Such an order would claim a parent sought custody or visitation and needed assistance in finding his or her children in order to bring the issue before a court.

*They are The Stolen Children Information Exchange, P.O. Box 465, Anaheim, California 92805; and Children's Rights of New York, Inc., 19 Maple Avenue, Stony Brook, New York 17790.

But this allows judges the option of *not* ordering the parent locator to find an absconding parent. A judge may decide that the stolen children have been gone long enough to be already in the custody of the absconding parent, and therefore there is no need for a custody hearing, no need to find the children.

Also, parents must hire lawyers to plead their cases. Most victimized parents are in the lower-middle-class income bracket and cannot afford such court suits.

The Department of Justice and the Federal Bureau of Investigation are fighting attempts to pass laws that make child stealing a federal responsibility. "We have consistently and vigorously opposed the federal criminalization of conduct involving the restraint of a minor child by his or her parent," says Mark Richard, deputy assistant attorney general of the Justice Department's Criminal Division. He feels it would be "inappropriate" to involve the federal criminal justice system in the area of domestic relations.

"Criminalization would place a severe strain on the resources of the FBI and the United States Attorney," he explains. "Sending the FBI to locate and arrest a parent may, in the case of an emotionally distraught parent, carry the potential for violence and, consequently, danger to the child."

Locally, many courts and police treat child stealing like wife abuse, claiming it is a domestic situation best left for civil authorities, not criminal investigation or prosecution.

When parents who have lost their children learn the government won't help, they become angry, then apathetic. But none of them forget their children. They are like families with servicemen missing in action: They feel their children are out there somewhere, but unreachable. They also feel defeated, embarrassed, even cheated, yet they haven't united. They could be a powerful lobby force. There are millions of parents who have been involved in child stealing,

either directly—by losing a child themselves—or indirectly
—by knowing a relative or friend who has lost a child or
children.

But they have no place to rally. Some write Congress,
where bills to make snatching a federal law have been introduced. Yet most parents shy away from politics. They feel it's
useless to protest, have no spirit for demonstrations or letter
writing. Their children have been stolen. What good is a law
that would not help them *now*? They want their families
back, their lives rebuilt.

Parents who steal children feel alienated, too. Some,
mostly fathers, feel judges and laws discriminate against
them. Mothers win custody much more frequently than fathers do. The only way they can see their children is to
steal them and hide.

But there are other motives for child stealing—revenge
and money. Many men and women are so embittered they
want to punish their former spouse. Even more, children
mean money. A parent with children doesn't pay child support. He or she gets it. A father might steal his son or daughter to avoid paying his ex-wife a weekly check. A mother
might steal children to receive that weekly check, either
from her former husband or the Department of Social Services.

Nobody wins with child stealing. Parents on the run with
stolen children lead nervous lives, use different names, look
over their shoulders constantly. Parents who have lost children suffer emotional and physical problems. And the children grow up unstable, questioning who they are, where the
other parent is, wondering why they can't use the telephone
or write home.

"No one can doubt that children kidnapped by a parent
suffer a great deal," says former Senator George McGovern,
a cosponsor of Senator Malcolm Wallop's bill to make child
stealing a federal crime. "The absence of a stable home environment is a difficult hurdle to overcome. The horrifying

experience of being kidnapped robs the child of this sense of security and permanence."

So both parents and children suffer. "Thousands of parents undergo tremendous heartache and anguish," Senator Alan Cranston says. "Thousands of innocent children are subjected to emotionally and psychologically damaging ordeals. Child snatching has, in fact, been described as a subtle form of child abuse."

Bills to make child stealing a federal crime have been introduced and subsequently tabled in Congress since 1973, when Congressman Charles Bennett sponsored a bill to remove the parental exemption clause from the kidnapping laws. Approximately twenty senators and fifty representatives have sponsored or cosponsored similar bills. One bill, drawn up by Senator Wallop, passed the Senate in 1978 and 1980. It died in the House Judiciary Committee's subcommittee on crime both years.

3

When It Happens

Parents steal children at all stages of marriage and divorce. They can also take them anytime during live-in situations, where parents aren't married. The clue is bitterness. A relationship sours. Parents fight. There might be drunkenness, wife abuse, nagging, arguments over money, or suspicions of adultery. This is when parents have to be careful about losing their children.

It depends upon how much hate there is. How much does one parent want to "get back at" the other parent? Marital becomes martial. But how martial? How much love has gone? How much anger has grown? Child stealing could signal the start of a divorce, or it could end a long court battle. It might happen the first day parents argue, or it might come years later. No one knows.

The FBI doesn't keep figures on how many child stealings there are each year. There are no statistics on how many parents steal children before custody hearings or after. There are no charts on how soon they steal children after a marriage or relationship crumbles, or begins to crumble. Child stealing might be the first sign of bitterness—a warning that one parent isn't happy—or it might be the last act of desperation or revenge.

There was a father in Texas who said he thought his marriage was fine. Then his wife said she wanted to work outside the home. The man, who owned a landscaping business in Houston, wouldn't allow it. But the woman insisted:

Their son had started first grade; she could have her old job back as a physical therapist; they needed extra money.

Her husband blew up. *He* would support his family, moonlight as a part-time private security guard at a local factory, two days a week, Saturday and Sunday.

"Why should you?" his wife asked. She was twenty-six. He was twenty-nine. She told him she could make more money for them. "Five days' pay is better than two," she said.

They fought over money one Sunday afternoon. They sent their son to a neighbor's home, argued through the afternoon football games. He didn't want to discuss it. She did. The Houston Oilers were on, his favorite team. They had season tickets. How could they use them if he worked weekends? she asked. She only wanted to help. He tried to ignore her. She turned off the television. "Listen to me," she said. "I'm bored all day."

"*I'll* pay the bills," he told her. "Besides, our son needs someone here when he comes home from school."

She said her friend could come over. He accused her of not wanting him anymore. Was she having an affair? Did she plan one? Who called first about her job? Did her boss call, or did she? The husband suspected that his wife went out with her boss before their marriage. Did she want to go out with him again? Did she want a divorce?

"I want new clothes for our son," she told him.

"*My* son," the man said.

He sulked for two hours. They didn't speak during the evening. He went out with his friends, came home late, woke her up. She was tired and ignored him. He took it as a final sign. In one short afternoon his marriage ended, he told her.

The next day he picked up their son after lunch from school, drove to a little town miles away, and called his wife from a motel. He wouldn't let her speak to the boy. "I'm not coming back unless you agree to stay home," he told her.

It was blackmail. But at least the abductor called and wanted to bargain, a good sign. The mother realized this, played her role. She begged her husband to return. She said it was a misunderstanding and agreed to what he wanted. He made her swear she wouldn't go back to her old job and wouldn't even call her former boss.

He drove up their driveway the next day. He'd kept his son barely twenty-four hours. But his leaving shook their marriage. Neither spouse was happy. They limped through two months, the husband threatening to steal their son again, the wife assuring him she would stay home. He felt scared, unconfident of his ability as a wage earner, jealous of his wife's ambition to work again. She felt helpless, a victim, trapped. She didn't want a divorce, but her husband was firm.

She was in a situation many parents face: They cannot prevent their children from being stolen unless they move, have legal custody, alert schools that *no one* other than the court-approved legal guardian can take their child or children home. She could have moved, but the courts might have seen that as a sign that she abandoned their marriage. Even if she took their son with her, she might have lost custody because her husband's lawyer might have argued that *she* stole the boy from his home.

"I thought about doing the same thing to my husband that *he* did to me," she said. "Leaving. I had my own car, but no job. What could I live on? Both my parents had passed away and I'd been an only child. Where could I go? I was a prisoner."

She didn't go anywhere. She thought of their child. "He shouldn't be taken on the road," she said. "First his daddy takes him, then his mommy takes him. He'd miss school and really likes his cub scout troop."

So, she stayed and endured. Her husband worked three weekends as a security guard, then quit. It was too much to work seven days a week. She became a bookkeeper and cashier in his landscaping business. She adjusted.

Mothers like this woman voice the same fears, especially if they are housewives. Some admit they would leave their husbands in situations like hers if they had money, a steady job, a relative or friend to move in with. They feel adrift, in need of support. Some venture into women's groups or centers for consciousness raising and counseling.

They do so at their own risk, they claim. Husbands who feel threatened by wives who seem too independent can panic. They sulk or argue. Child stealing is one of their options, they say. "If you get too independent, you'll never see your children again," they preach. This threat often follows other threats to take the house, clean out the bank account, and refuse to pay alimony if there is a divorce.

Other mothers aren't so lucky. They can't adjust. They can't reconcile after the first argument about their marriage with its caution about child stealing. A San Francisco mother lost her child—a seven-year-old daughter—and she never found her. There was a fight over whether she was faithful and her husband left, taking their child with him. Reasons for husbands or wives leaving can vary. There might be fights over money, affairs, or the spouse's life-style and values.

When child stealing occurs in the early stages of divorce, it can be final because there is no divorce settlement yet and no child custody arrangement. One Chicago mother *still* doesn't know where her daughter and husband are. She isn't aware if she's still married or if he got a divorce in some other state. There's no way for her to find out with official help from the government because there are no legal papers. She doesn't have a custody order that was violated.

Some parents lose their children *after* divorce, where there *is* a custody order. They generally have better luck at recovering their children. They may obtain a felony warrant if they live in one of the thirty or so states that treat child stealing as a felony. However, this doesn't mean police or sheriffs will look for their children. It usually means the authorities will arrest an alleged abductor if he or she is found.

A father or mother who steals their children after a court hearing usually is still angry. The motives are the same as for someone who does it *before* a hearing: revenge, money, frustration with the courts and laws. Only it hasn't surfaced. Sometimes a spouse hopes the courts will punish a former partner, but sees it hasn't happened, and decides to take the law into his or her own hands. However, a parent might use the children to forge a better agreement about money or custody out of court now that a judge has ruled against him or her.

"I'm not paying the alimony, and if you try to enforce it, I'll take the kids," a divorced father from Cleveland, Ohio, told his ex-wife. She wouldn't let him see their three children and was afraid he would steal them. He didn't pay and there was a standoff, what fathers call the "no see, no pay" situation. Mothers call it "no pay, no see." These cases are ones of child *restraint*, not stealing. One parent knows where his or her children are, but can't see them, or doesn't want to see them. Either parent can strike first—the mother holding back on weekend visitation, or the father holding back support checks. Either parent may go back into court first, too, asking to enforce weekly visits or payments. And either way only one parent sees the children.

But it can go further. Suppose the father pays and the mother allows him weekend visits. He may not return his children Sunday night, which is how most parents abduct them. Courts give times of day and days of the week to visit. The custodial parent generally lives up to the order and lets the children go, often never to see them again.

Or they could be stolen over a summer visit, when the noncustodial parent has them for a month or so. Children fly from coast to coast. They call the parent at home during July and August. Everything seems fine. They'll even say when they're coming home. The noncustodial parent will call and give a flight number, an airline name, a date, a time. The other parent drives to the airport, relieved, summer's tension dissipating. But the children don't get off the plane. The parent checks with the airline, learns they weren't on the flight, calls the former spouse. Sometimes they talk. "I'm not returning them," the parent with summer visitation rights says. Or, his or her phone goes unanswered. There might have been a change of numbers. An operator says there's a new listing, unpublished. There might be a letter in the next day or two: "The children are fine. They've decided to live with me." Summer nightmares come true.

One mother from San Luis Obispo, California, sent her two sons to Long Island, New York, in July 1979. Her former husband was a stockbroker on Wall Street. But he left his job in August and went on the road with the boys. The mother called his relatives, who said they didn't know where he was. New York had given her custody and California, upholding that order, gave her a felony warrant. Police on Long Island talked to the man's relatives and friends. They all told them what they'd told the mother: We don't know where he and the children are.

Luckily, the man ran out of money. He'd worked as a carpenter and had driven to Georgia in a camper, then put his sons into school in Florida. He put them on a plane to Kennedy Airport one Sunday night in March 1980.

Parents with custody claim they uphold legal agreements or orders about visitation, but still lose their children. Their former spouses charge they'll take them to court for contempt, have them fined, or even jailed, if they don't send the children for the summer or for a weekend.

Yet sometimes when custodial parents do allow former spouses to visit, they can lose their children. These custodial parents have upheld the law, sent their children for visits. But the noncustodial parents sometimes don't uphold the law and won't return the children. Parents with custody then feel cheated. They lost their children by upholding legally ordered visitation agreements or decrees. But they might not get police or district attorneys to help them find and recover their children. In short, they upheld the law and lost. Now the law won't help them. Their ex-spouses *broke* the law and can hide without fear that law enforcement agencies will hunt for them.

Both parents with custody and visitation claim their papers are worth nothing without the FBI or police to search for their children and enforce their orders.

"Why spend so much money on lawyers and courts if what they decide doesn't matter?" the mother in San Luis Obispo asked.

Which is why some parents take children *before* court hearings. "Why bother?" one father in Dallas said. "I'd rather spend my money buying clothes or traveling with my kids."

Unmarried parents have the most trouble. They have birth certificates, nothing else. They still can go into court and receive an order appointing them legal guardians of their children. Their papers would serve as custody orders, which might be violated if their former partners took their children.

Yet children stolen from unmarried parents are taken *before* either partner has tried any court action. Courts don't like to decide custody between married or unmarried parents without the children being there. Parents have to lie and claim their sons or daughters have *not* been taken and that their former partner abandoned them and they want to protect against child stealing. This means their attorneys will have to commit perjury, too, claiming their clients have the children at home.

Losing and recovering children can depend on when these unmarried parents separate. Sometimes the father will move out while the expecting mother is pregnant. He won't be there when the child is born. The mother could claim the father is unknown, and have the birth certificate say that. Or, she just might write in "unstated," which still leaves the father off the birth certificate.

If he steals the child, he would be kidnapping him or her. The Lindbergh Law would apply in this case. It states that a person is a kidnapper who "unlawfully seizes, confines, inveigles, decoys, kidnaps, abducts, or carries away and holds for ransom or reward or otherwise any person, except in the case of a minor by the parent thereof." The FBI would look for that child, as long as the mother never says it was the father who made the abduction.

Often the woman wants nothing to do with her former lover. Yet she might list him on the birth certificate to get child support. She has the option of money or safety for her child. If she does list the father, she could risk losing her child by abduction if he wanted to punish her or save the child support. She'd be safer if she didn't list him, and did not claim child support. Some unwed parents do this anyway so the woman can receive welfare.

But unwed mothers don't think of child stealing while pregnant. They often see the child as a way to keep lovers —emotionally, financially, physically. They want them to know they are fathers. Men who are angry at them will often leave before the baby arrives. And the mother may be so furious she might list the father's name in order to have the state welfare department come after him. She might not even want the money. She wants the man and will use the threat of child support payments—liens on the father's salary, attachments on his property—to bring him home. If he does what she wants, he may get out of paying because she might withdraw her claims for welfare.

Unwed parents don't think about child stealing that much. They might threaten to take a child before they'd actually do it. But they'd do it when the relationship soured.

And it does happen.

Marilyn Cifilli was twenty-one, lived in New York City,

and stayed with her boyfriend for two years. He left soon after their baby, a girl, Dawn, was born in 1978. His parents didn't like Marilyn, said she was too radical, too modern in her thinking. They first claimed their son, Richard Howard, wasn't Dawn's father. But Richard's mother, Dawn's grandmother, changed her mind. She wanted the baby after a year. Marilyn allowed her to see the child, even though the grandmother claimed not to know where Richard was.

Marilyn lived in Greenwich Village. Richard Howard's mother lived in Queens. The baby went out for a weekend once and didn't come back. Marilyn called; there was no answer. She went to the house; there was no one home. Richard called her two days later and said he and his parents had moved to Florida, where they'd raise Dawn in sunny suburbia.

"I was shocked already," Marilyn said. "It'd been a year since I'd heard his voice. I couldn't imagine what was happening. Richie was a stranger to Dawn."

Marilyn had a friend who knew a lawyer. But she didn't have any money. She soon learned the Howards had sold their house. Their attorney handled their affairs and wouldn't say where in Florida the family had settled.

Marilyn had put Richard Howard's name on Dawn's birth certificate and learned that he'd gotten a copy of it from the Board of Health several weeks before his parents stole Dawn. She saved some money and went to Miami, where Richard had once said he had relatives.

She looked in the phone book. There were dozens of Howards in Dade County. It was useless, so many names, so few leads. She gave up and returned to New York.

Now she is studying to be a legal secretary at the New School for Social Research. She'd been a waitress and now is a secretary at a small manufacturing firm.

"I haven't given up," she said. "But I have my life. Someday, maybe, I'll find Dawn. Even if it takes moving to Florida, or wherever."

Marilyn Cifilli's case points out how unmarried parents are more vulnerable to child stealing than married ones. She couldn't get a court order appointing her legal guardian of her daughter because she didn't do so *before* the father took their child. Also, Dawn's birth certificate had Richard Howard's name on it.

Cifilli wanted to get legal custody of her child, but couldn't because the child wasn't with her. She wasn't able to obtain any court papers that she then could take to the police and show how her ex-lover had violated them.

When parents are unmarried, occasionally the instigation for stealing children comes from grandparents, as in Marilyn Cifilli's case. Often they disapprove of the young parents' life-style and are convinced they can provide the child with a better environment than the actual parents. Usually they aid fathers. Their sons marry, have children, divorce. Grandparents either want their grandchildren to live with them or feel former daughters-in-law won't let them visit. Or, they're afraid their former daughters-in-law will steal their grandchildren. So they lean on their sons to take their children before their wives can do it. They want the babies, whether the natural parents were married or not. They'll help finance trips and will move themselves to be near the stolen children. Some claim their former daughters-in-law unfit; others say they just want to raise children again.

Grandparents with money can support their sons and grandchildren. Often their sons are weak, and need a parent to order their lives, or they don't really want their children, but will steal them if their parents help. Richard Howard didn't see his daughter, but his mother did. He'd abandoned his child until his mother and father decided to retire in Florida and his mother felt *she* could raise Dawn better than Marilyn Cifilli. There was a religious and life-style conflict involved here, too.

Grandparents sometimes steal grandchildren because they feel their *own* children are unfit parents. They usually object to the way their children live. Grandparents are often concerned that their grandchildren are being harmfully exposed to drugs, alcohol, and sex. A mother and daughter will fight over how to raise babies. The mother will speak with her husband. Both agree their daughter and her husband don't know what they're doing with the children. They must do something, they say. So they steal their grandchildren, move out of state to hide from the police and the child's natural parents. If they are out of state, they can't be arrested for custodial interference except on a felony warrant. And it can be just as hard to get a felony warrant on grandparents as it is to get one on parents.

Parents who want to recover children from grandparents can, after finding them, serve a writ of habeas corpus with a writ of attachment on the abducting grandparents and have the children brought into court. Judges will usually give children to parents rather than to grandparents or relatives.

If the grandparents or relatives still want the children, they'll have to prove the natural parents unfit, ask for an investigation of the home, complain to child protective agencies, and take the parents to court.

Grandparents or relatives *might* have a chance at winning custody if the natural parents are divorced and they can prove that their life-style, with two parents, a secure income and home, is better than the life-style of a broke single parent.

Most custody fights between parents and grandparents happen when the natural parents aren't married. Grandparents might charge that the parents are immoral, that they shouldn't have had children if they only lived together, or that they should have married once the mother became pregnant.

Judges might agree and take a child away from its natural mother. Usually, however, they don't, unless there are extreme circumstances, hard evidence that the mother is unfit

—leaving children unattended, abusing them, having different men sleep over.

Grandparents become frustrated. They feel the courts haven't realized how bad a parent an unwed mother is. It doesn't matter whether she is their child or not. They want to step in, take control.

Sometimes unwed mothers will give up their children for adoption. Sometimes they'll keep them, but have their parents raise them, at least for a while. And then the grandparents won't give them back. There have been mothers who had to take their own parents to court and force them to hand over the children. Taking grandparents to court can be easy, because they don't move as much, are older, perhaps retired.

Ida Swartz, sixty-two, a retired secretary, and her husband, a retired truck driver, moved from Long Island to Orlando, Florida, in 1978. They took their grandson with them. "We didn't like how he was being raised," she said. "He was only three years old and had been burned several times already—water from the stove, cigarettes, things like that."

The boy's mother was Ida Swartz's daughter. "I guess I should blame myself," Swartz said. "It was my own daughter who was raising the boy. But we couldn't ignore the situation, my husband and I. My daughter needed her own life and we'd talked about it. But she didn't want to give us legal custody."

Her daughter wasn't married, and hadn't listed the child's father on the birth certificate. Everyone knew who he was, though. But no one wanted to have anything to do with him.

"He was a bum," Swartz said. "My daughter lived with him when she was nineteen and should have been going to college. She went to him, instead. It was a rebellion kind of thing."

Their daughter lived in Brooklyn, shared an apartment

with another unwed mother. They lived on welfare. "It was filthy," Swartz said. "We wanted to give our grandson a lawn, a backyard. But she wouldn't give him up. I think she didn't want to lose her welfare. My husband and I are on pensions and didn't want to give her any money, even if we could. If she's not going to school, she should go to work."

They took their grandson after a weekend visit. They went to Orlando and bought a home in a trailer camp. They told their daughter where they were, though, said they'd hired a lawyer in Florida and would fight for custody. Their daughter had no money for court costs.

"We told her she could come live with us," Swartz said. "We'd told her that on Long Island and after we moved, too. But she wouldn't have it. So now we have a nice little boy who's close to Disneyworld."

If fathers feel slighted by divorce and custody laws, unmarried fathers have it worse. First, they have to find their children (again), then prove they are the father, then ask for visitation or custody. Faced with legal battles, they often steal children.

But if unwed mothers steal children, they might get away with it more easily. There is the problem of hiding, of course. But if they're found, they'll probably retain custody, unless they want to put up their children for adoption.

Then the fathers will have a chance. Better to leave a child with a natural parent, they argue, than with strangers.

But fathers, and mothers, too, fear their children will be adopted without their knowing about it. There is no way of telling how many stolen children, particularly those of unwed parents, end up in foster homes or with adoptive families.

4

The Father's Perspective

A majority of children are snatched by fathers. Most male child stealers claim they had no alternative. They feel that the laws were written to favor mothers. And that judges and government agencies perpetuate that prejudice by not enforcing fathers' visitation rights while scrupulously enforcing child support payments.

It is vague custody orders and the unwillingness of judges to enforce them that encourage fathers to steal their children. Some custody orders say nothing more than that the husband and wife should work out a mutually agreeable custody arrangement. Others say fathers can see their children for only one day a week. Some judges list hours of the day when children are allowed out with their dads. Other judges say visitation can be one day a week and a Saturday overnight every other weekend.

As a result, men feel alienated. Once they lived with their children. Now custody papers have reduced them to visitors and guests, like out-of-town relatives. They feel they aren't parents anymore, just paying guardians, their salaries watched closely by ex-wives, their children growing up without strong masculine role models.

Over and above this, there is the question of money, which makes them even angrier. The same courts that offer no help in arranging to see their children punish them for falling behind on child support. A mother can move, leave the state, not say where she is going. The father suddenly finds the county probation department after him, ordering him to send support monies to them, not directly to his ex-wife. But when the father asks where his children are, probation officers refuse to help. Some fathers have taken in their visitation orders and have had court clerks actually laugh at them. They tell the men to find their wives, bring them to court in the new state, or fly them home to the old one.

But these men don't know where their wives are. How can they bring them to court? Besides, they'd have to hire lawyers to do that. Perhaps they'd have to pay for their ex-wife's lawyer, too, which chafes even more.

One man who found no help from the legal establishment was Gary Rice. He was forced to take the law into his own hands to recover his son. A thirty-four-year-old stockbroker in Chicago, he lost his son twice to his former wife. He claimed to have had the law on his side both times he recovered his boy, Karl, who was five years old.

Rice's wife took their son to Brooklyn early in 1977, just after the couple separated. There were no custody papers yet. He hired a private investigator, learned where his wife lived, and picked up his son off the street. Rice said he wanted their son returned to Illinois because he felt his case should be decided there.

"I didn't want to go into court in a second state, especially New York," he said.

There was a hearing in Chicago in spring 1977, and a judge gave Rice's wife temporary custody of Karl, with visitation rights to Gary.

But his wife went east a second time, right after that hearing, to stay with her parents again. Rice said he tried for months to see his son, but couldn't.

"I came back in October [1977] and they didn't even

open the door," he said. "Then I came back a few days later with photographs and tape recordings to show I was in New York."

Rice went into court in Chicago that November. His wife didn't appear. He showed the judge his plane tickets and said he couldn't even speak with his son, or see him. He had tape recordings of himself at his former wife's door in Brooklyn. He'd also taped telephone calls to her.

"I had called them up and said, 'I'd like to speak with my son' and they'd tell me he wasn't in. I'd ask where he was and tell them this was his father calling. I'd ask my mother-in-law where my son was and she said she was the maid and couldn't give out any information."

After that, a Chicago judge gave him custody. But he still didn't have his child. So he hired John Raleigh, thirty-eight, of Belmont, New York, to help recover his boy a second time. Raleigh was one of several "custody vigilantes" who worked in the United States at that time. "Nobody wanted Karl more than I when I went to New York in the spring [1978]," Rice said. "I hadn't seen him for a year and I had an opportunity to get him a week earlier. I had followed my wife, her parents, and Karl to a park and had three other guys with me. We were less than five yards behind them. They walked in a parking lot and we didn't try it because his grandmother and grandfather were each holding one of his hands. To have tried it could possibly have broken his arm.

"I was following them around for a couple of weeks and didn't have many opportunities," he said. Raleigh had told him a cardinal rule in child snatching: Never take the first chance—wait, watch, don't be hasty.

"If you take the first opportunity and it's not good, it might be the last you'll ever get," Rice said.

He had a map and his route out of New York planned, he said. There were several places he could stay. There was a police radio in the getaway car so he could hear if there was a bulletin out for him, and he had several escape plans. His wife didn't know any of the people who were with him, and she didn't know any of the places he might hide afterward, he explained.

One weekend evening he saw his son, his wife, and his in-laws come out of a restaurant. "Karl was running a few feet in front of them," Rice said. "I went up behind them and one of my guys ran up from the front and cut between them and the child. They were startled and pulled back when they saw him coming.

"Then I came from behind and grabbed Karl. My fear was that they would react in defense and throw themselves on top of him and then it would have been impossible. Sheer fright took over and they didn't act, at first. I picked up the child and ran to the middle of the street. The next thing that happened, one of the guys tried to get back to his car. My wife's father went after him and had his arms around him and tried to get him out of that car.

"We were trying to pull her father from there. The next thing we knew Mace was sprayed in the guy's car. Her father pulled off the glasses of one of our other guys and sprayed Mace in his face. We *all* tried to get into that car— me, Karl, my guys, her father. We finally pulled him out, but that Mace was everywhere.

"Karl was crying for about two hours and our eyes burned something terrible for a few hours. We had trouble seeing to drive. When it wore off, Karl stopped crying. It was a rented car we left in, paid in cash, and I didn't return it. I just left it on the street a few blocks away, got into the second car, and called the rental company to tell them where their car was."

Rice claimed his former wife and her family spent about $70,000 on lawyers. He said it made him bitter. "When I look at my own financial situation and think about all the money I have had to spend, all because she wouldn't let me know my kid, I have no sympathy for her," he said.

Still, he had mixed feelings. "I really don't like this situation," he said. "I honestly believe that this child should see his mother. But she's responsible for her own mess. I'm not thrilled with the situation, but I don't see what the alternative is."

So he disappeared, with another child "lost" or "stolen," unable to see both parents. Rice didn't come to other court hearings because he didn't want anyone to know where he lived. He also felt he'd never get a fair trial; that he'd *had* to "steal" his son twice; that his ex-wife would vanish with Karl, too, if she had the chance.

His ex-wife won custody of their son about a year later because of Rice's disappearance. But she doesn't have Karl. No one knows where he and his father are now.

There is an economic side to fathers' rights. Many men find themselves paying child support but not seeing their children. And while there are federal agencies (the Parent Locator Service) that will track down fathers for alimony and child support payments, there is no service to enforce visitation rights. The frustration and economic drain this causes, without the reward of seeing their children, leads many men to steal children.

"Often a father can't see his children and the mother does everything she can—hides out, changes her name, moves around—and this society of ours does everything it can to collect money for her. All the officials care about is money, even though they know these kids need a father, too," said Sloane Culkin, fifty-four, who's been active for over five years with a California-based "fathers' rights" group.

"I've got a circular view on child snatching," he said. While he officially doesn't like it, he doesn't blame men who did it after their wives left with their children.

"When this happens and a guy snatches his kids, I say, 'Great, good for you.' I don't blame the father, I blame the mother, because she started the ball rolling. As long as a kid has to have one parent or the other, and as long as a guy has the guts enough to grab his kid, then I say more power to him."

One father who found himself paying a considerable amount in child support without having his visitation rights enforced is Don Clevenger. He spoke for many fathers in saying the Federal Parent Locator Service should search for children as well as collect money.

"We want the correct use of the Federal Parent Locator Service, or else to change its name to a collection agency. That's all it is," he said.

He spoke for both fathers *and* mothers when he told how many of the government's offices don't help victimized parents. Clevenger, thirty-nine, is a computer services consultant. His ex-wife, thirty-eight, is a hairdresser. The couple married in 1970. In August 1978, Clevenger moved out of their home in Silver Spring, Maryland, and his wife changed the locks. She claimed he beat her. But she didn't show for a brutality hearing in October 1978, and charges against him were dropped.

She allowed him to see their daughter and son on weekends. But Clevenger charged she threw their daughter against a wall, injuring her head. A Virginia court awarded him custody of his two children, plus twenty dollars a month in child support. His ex-wife tried then to win custody in Maryland and Iowa, but those states had enacted uniform custody laws (which meant they would recognize Virginia's decree) and wouldn't hear her case. So she snatched the children from their Virginia school and went to Washington State, which ignored Virginia's order, gave custody to her, and ordered him to pay child support.

Like many fathers, Clevenger finds himself paying child support to another state, and yet he can't see his children. "The judge here said he can't order visitation because my ex-wife is out of his jurisdiction. He *did* order me to pay child support because of the Uniform Reciprocal Enforcement of Support Act, though."

The existing federal law helps states find fathers to pay money to mothers. It lets district attorneys and other officials use computers in the Internal Revenue Service to find out how much a man earns. County child support enforcement agencies track these men down. But, again, their only interest is in money, not children. This policy works against a mother who has lost children, too. She can go to an enforcement agency for child support, but if she says her ex-husband took their children, she won't get help.

Clevenger claims that the state of Washington never told him there was a hearing on custody, and that the court in Virginia that collects the child support won't tell him where they send his money. It is three hundred dollars a month.

"I don't mind paying, but I resent not seeing the children," he said. Washington has since adopted uniform custody, but it doesn't help. "The court in Washington said the court in Virginia was not a court of record and since my children were in Washington they were in that state's jurisdiction, regardless of the Uniform Child Custody Jurisdiction Act."

Clevenger feels helpless and broke. "I was unable to pursue fighting for custody," he said, "because I was always notified *after* their court dates had passed. I was first notified she got custody in Washington, for instance, on December 27, 1978, a month after the actual hearing."

He has spent $30,000 on his fight. "I just had a notice from an attorney out there that I owe him eleven hundred dollars," he said. "I don't have it."

Clevenger explained that what many fathers feel is an inequality in the divorce system—the government will come after them for money, but will do nothing to find their children.

"I am presently ordered to pay child support," he said, "for the children I have custody of." But his wife has refused to give him her address or telephone number. "Grandparents pay for this, too," he said. "Friends, other relatives. It is very emotional. My parents do not know where they [his children] are. They have not had any contact, either, for fifteen months."

He doesn't want to send money to the County Child Protection Agency in Washington, he explained. He wants to send it directly to his ex-wife and be able to see his children. "I would pay," Clevenger said to a public hearing in Washington, D.C., on proposed bills to curb child stealing. "But where do I send it? I will go to jail first, me, a law-abiding citizen.

"I believe in the law. Most of the members of the groups I belong to believe in the law. My knees tremble when I go before a judge."

Clevenger would prefer to have a government agency enforce custody arrangements rather than having to resort to "self-help" or "vigilante" recoveries.

"How about the violence of an amateur who goes in and snatches his kid?" he asked. "How about the number of children who have died in this manner? How about the child abuse?

"I would rather have a professional going in. I would rather have some help figuring out where I paid the money to see my kids. Even after I find my kids, I can't visit them."

In regard to the cost his plan will incur, he had this to say at the hearing: "We heard this morning that it would cost a lot of money when the FBI and the Justice Department and the Parent Locator become involved. How about the money *I* have spent? How about the money the other one hundred thousand or so people last year spent and the *next* one hundred thousand are going to spend?

"I wouldn't mind paying a little more in taxes if I could find a responsive government that was more concerned with love than with the mere collection of money, personal greed, and profit," Clevenger said.

He has worked to have the Uniform Custody Act passed in Virginia and counsels parents who have lost their children. He wants to do all he can to stop child snatching and joined Parents Without Partners, which backs the Wallop and Bennett bills to make snatching a federal crime, Big Brothers, Offenders Aid, and Parents Aides of Fairfax County.

"We're not going to change laws by sitting around saying that everything is terrible," he said. "Are we going to make it better for our sons and daughters? Are we even going to have a voice in raising them before they grow up and have children of their own? I'm in favor of S.105 [Senator Wallop's bill]. It would have helped me at the time my wife left. It would even help me now, if I could get a court order for visitation.

"I have a number of friends who can't see their children, and one of the provisions in S.105 is for visitation, which we desperately need. Now, even if I get a court order for visitation, my ex-wife doesn't have to recognize it. She can say the children are sick every time I turn up. I think S.105 would enforce my visitation and allow me to find and see my children."

5

Fathers' Rights Groups

Some men have started groups to champion their rights as
fathers. Most are fighting for the passage of joint custody
laws, where the legal rights to children after divorce would
be shared. Some, more defeatist, simply urge fathers to steal
their children; others oppose child snatching. There are
about two hundred groups, mostly in California and New
York.* And they are angry.

"From a male point of view, county courts have a notori-
ous and infamous reputation," says George Doppler, fifty-
three, a fathers' rights leader from Pennsylvania who claims
to have counseled more than five thousand men in his thirteen years in fathers' rights. "Most child custody court ses-
sions are a farce, just window dressing to make the male
parent think he has had his day in court, which in most cases
is a sham."

He feels child stealing is a problem because fathers aren't
treated fairly by divorce laws. Politicians should change
those laws and give fathers a chance to live with their children.

Doppler explains that in some states fathers are awarded
custody in only 2 percent of the cases; in other states it
might be 6 percent. "These statistics alone should tell the
world the child custody system in the United States is sick.

*The two most active fathers' rights groups are: United Fathers Organiza-
tion of America, Inc., P.O. Box 8451, Fountain Valley, CA 92708, 714-962-
8046; and Equal Rights for Fathers, P.O. Box 546, Rochester, N.Y. 14602,
716-482-9922.

"With conditions like this, and the attitudes of society like this, many fathers are not going to stay around and wait for some court to take their children from them. They are going to take their kids and run. I have come to learn that there is a certain group of parents who think that once their marriage has turned bad the other parent is to have nothing to do with the children except to send money," he says.

"When this is the female parent she has two legal means to enable her to move to any part of the United States and still collect her child support: the Uniform Reciprocal Enforcement of Support Act and the Federal Enforcement of Support Act."

These laws help mothers in one state get child support from fathers in other states. URESA is a federal law which enables states to enforce one another's child support orders. FESA, also a federal law, provides funds to help states collect the child support. They are sore points with men, who sometimes feel the government only wants their money and doesn't care about their children.

"I can think of no two other legal instruments which are encouraging child snatching and so effectively destroying the association with the other parent," he says.

Doppler's views go deep into the system itself, however, a legal system he considers one-sided and cruel: "What we're up against in this country is the annihilation by the American judicial system of the relationship between children and their fathers when parents divorce."

Weak visitation orders, strong child support orders, are yokes that bring fathers screaming into group meetings in Los Angeles, California, and Rochester, New York. They see their children and their money vanishing, claim to believe in the law, and point the evil finger at mothers. They all praise families, damn deserting parents, wrap themselves in cloaks of trust and affection. *They* wouldn't run out on their kids, they say, or hide from support orders. They love their children too much and don't mind paying. And they resent the claim many women make that men only want custody in order to avoid paying weekly child support checks.

So they meet, draft newsletters, write politicians, sometimes picket courthouses. Their leaders are divorced men like George Doppler, fathers who've come to the movement through personal experience. Most of them have had a bad divorce, are having trouble seeing their sons and daughters, and want to do something about it—change laws, counsel other men, vent their anger in public gatherings rather than in private pubs.

One of the more active leaders in New York State is Garry Brown, forty, a machine builder in Rochester, New York. He started Equal Rights for Fathers in November 1976, and has advised between fifteen hundred and two thousand people since then, he said. His group has eight chapters around the state, a monthly newsletter, and weekly meetings. Current issues of their publication list bills in the state legislature on joint custody and divorce reform which these fathers like.

"It wasn't until after my divorce that I found out a custodial parent has absolute and total right to set visitation," Brown said. Divorced in 1969, he had trouble seeing his children.

"I didn't have their phone number, no school records, no medical records. I could see them on a weekly basis," he said, "but there was always a hassle. It was supposed to be during the day, on Saturdays. I worked Saturdays, though, and it was difficult. My children were three, eight, and nine at the time. I was told by my lawyer that I couldn't get them legally. A child psychologist also told me there was no possible way I could get them. For eleven years I couldn't call them on the phone. I didn't have the number. About a year ago the kids gave me their number, but asked me not to call there. If I tried to involve myself in their lives, the kids got hell."

Brown's group sent a letter to divorced fathers asking

them to write to their state legislators about bills in Albany that deal with men's issues. He believes child stealing starts in legal centers—county courts, mostly—which create situations where frustrated men shatter before indifferent judges with their unsympathetic visitation orders.

"The motivation for child snatching begins in the courtroom or probation department after a marriage dissolves," Brown said. "Since sole custody is practically a reward, presumed in the best interest of children, the losing parent is deprived of the right of parenthood. This can take the form of denial of visitation, and can be ego-shattering. It may be dealt with by retaliation, such as child snatching, depression, or the neurotic acceptance of the loss of the child, as though he or she had died.

"Children need and love both parents after a divorce and both parents must be permitted to play an active role in their development."

Active roles are what men want. When they don't get them, they may take situations into their own hands—which means child stealing.

It happened to Joseph Paul, thirty-two, who runs a sporting goods store in upstate New York. He couldn't see his son, so he took him for a few months, then decided against hiding out, and returned and joined Equal Rights for Fathers.

But Joe Paul is different. He's angry, yet feels he shouldn't keep his boy from his mother. He is one of the few parents who came out of the woods voluntarily, and who now fights for other fathers. He's become an activist.

"We're very concerned about rights for fathers in terms of what's best for the children," Paul said. "We feel children are not getting a fair shake, especially when one parent can call the shots and eliminate the other parent. This inequity stems from women getting custody most of the time, and we're trying to get something done about it."

He feels that mothers abuse their powers too much. "It's the abuse of custodial powers that forces people into this situation. The noncustodial parent doesn't have any recourse," Paul said. "We need laws to help the noncustodial parent when there is interference with visitation rights.

"The New York State judiciary still views the father as a secondary parent, to be divorced from his children as well as from his wife," Paul explained. He said that taking a child away from one parent creates trauma for that child and hurts him or her in school.

Paul feels it costs too much for a father to try for custody, even if he can prove a mother abuses her custodial power. "The present system, which gives mothers so much power in terms of child custody and money, puts the noncustodial parent—the father—in a position where he has to spend five to ten thousand dollars that he doesn't have to get even a small recourse by going to court."

Joseph Paul found himself in exactly that position. His wife met a new man and wanted out. They had one child, a son, Edward, who was five years old when they separated in 1976. Paul gave his wife custody and didn't hire a lawyer. He trusted his wife, he said. There was no mention of when he could see Eddie, or for how long, in their divorce order.

"I thought I could trust her word," he said. "At the time we had a nice duplex apartment in Rochester, where I was a bacteriologist for the city water department. I was in hock keeping her in clothes. Then she met this rich guy she wanted to marry and asked for a divorce. Three weeks after she met him, he bought her an eighteen-thousand-dollar Mercedes.

"She felt that if she could force me out of the picture, she wouldn't have to deal with me. She had two friends in the same position. They gave their husbands a little flak about seeing the kids and the husbands just took off, never came around again. She figured that's the way all husbands were.

"When we went to her lawyer, he said she had no grounds and there was no way she could get a divorce. She and her friend made their plans and even built a house. They asked me to help them [get her a divorce so they could marry]. I told her point-blank, 'You know what is important to me. My son. If you can guarantee that he won't be interfered with, I don't see any problem.' I told them I wouldn't contest the divorce if they *both* promised not to interfere with my relationship with him. Part of that agreement was that they wouldn't ask for child support and I would agree to pay for his college education.

"That was our basic verbal agreement. Then the whole thing completely fell apart as soon as she got married again. I would call and ask to see my son and they would tell me it wasn't convenient."

Paul found it became difficult to see his son. "I asked for him every weekend and they told me that since I wasn't paying support, I couldn't keep him overnight," he said. "I told them we had an agreement and they said it wasn't good anymore. From that point on things went downhill. They decided that in the best interest of Eddie, he wouldn't see me at all. That's when I got a lawyer."

Paul went to court and after three months had a temporary injunction to see his son. "I was left with having him every other Saturday for five hours," Paul said. "So I went back to court. She [his former wife] delayed, first saying she was pregnant, then that she was breast-feeding a new baby," he said.

Paul became angry and depressed, and felt helpless. "After two years of not seeing my son for more than five hours every two weeks, after first trying to negotiate with them and then trying to get them into court, I felt my chances slimmer and slimmer. My son was growing up without me. Time was running out. They stopped at nothing to keep me from seeing him. It wasn't healthy.

"I was losing contact with him. We were drifting further and further apart. You don't build a parent-child relationship once every two weeks for five hours.

"I decided that if one of us was going to be left out of the parenting process, I would take steps to see it wasn't me. My first desire was that we could share him equally and give him the best of both of us. That seemed impossible," Paul said.

He realized then that he should have hired a lawyer *before* his divorce and had his rights to see his son protected. There was only one way out.

In March 1978, Joseph Paul snatched his son.

"I felt driven to what I did," he said. "They brought him over for my five hours and I went to Buffalo, took a plane to California, and then a train to Oregon. I had a suitcase in one hand and my son in the other and we started from scratch.

"I took a part-time job listed on the student employment board at a university there. It turned out to be an assembly line job in a small factory. Oregon was interesting to me because of its ecological and environmental thinking. Another thing I wanted was the life of a small college town with a large university. I registered under a different name and got my student ID card and was all set. I figured the educational climate would be good and my son's schooling top-notch."

Paul enjoyed being a full-time parent. "I put Eddie in school there and went to parent-teacher meetings and talked with his teachers. It was extremely satisfying. For once I was involved with my son's upbringing. I saw what he did in class and knew how well he did. You know, report cards and homework. It was fun, the happiest three and a half months of my life.

"Eddie was just as happy as I. If it had been bad for him, I wouldn't have done it. I knew how close our relationship was and what it meant to both of us. I was very, very sure in my mind that I wasn't harming him."

Joseph Paul, who likes children and Frisbees and fresh air, was trying to be a good parent, but realized his son should have a mother. "The more I thought about it, the more I realized I was doing exactly what I had complained my wife had done to *me*. It wasn't the right thing. I discussed it with my lawyer and we decided that in the very long run, I should come back and work it out, however long it took. Go through those damn courts and get something squared away.

"I spoke with my former wife over the phone and told her to grant me visitation rights while we worked this out. My lawyer said there was no way I could get anything on paper while I was away. They would consider it coercion. She agreed over the phone that she hadn't been fair, that I could see Eddie whenever I wanted from now on, and that it was partly their fault.

"So I went back and they took him and I haven't seen him since Christmas," Paul said. "I called at Easter to say 'Happy Easter' and they wouldn't even let me speak to him."

Though many fathers' rights groups urge men to stand and fight, to work within the system, there is a small men's group that has abandoned the law altogether. They live "underground" and often steal children for other men.

According to Hiram Belforte, thirty-nine, the editor of a small magazine for fathers' rights in Texas, "I can understand why they're underground. Some owe five or ten thousand dollars in back alimony and child support. They have good jobs now, mostly off-the-books."

And they help one another. Belforte, who claims to be one of the underground network's founders, said that he knows of four men, mostly in western states, who have lists of other men who will put up fathers on the run. "Nobody has written lists, of course," he said. "We keep names and addresses in our heads, and each guy knows only a limited number of other guys. That way, if one of us goes to court and the government has proof we know about each other, we're only compromising four guys each.

"This is a highly militant organization," he pointed out. "I know personally that it's into child stealing as well as hiding guys. It may have killed four people [while taking kids], but I don't know about them directly."

Belforte, a car salesman and weekend bartender, explained that the group has no more than twenty or thirty members and has a floating headquarters. "Its members don't work," he said. "They live off the land out west and camp out like rural guerrillas. I'm one of the few who has a straight job. Their motive is strictly to work on divorce and custody cases and they try to recruit other men to join them."

The group started in San Antonio, Texas, and Vancouver, British Columbia, and has stolen about twenty-five children, he estimates. Apparently, it's coordinated, taking children out of at least two provinces in Canada, and possibly a third, and shipping the Canadian children into at least three states in the United States. It hides divorced men and their children and gives them false papers.

Its members like rural areas, where most of them can find work on farms or driving trucks. Many are carpenters, masons, house painters, bartenders, waiters, cooks. They can't work in white-collar jobs, which they once did, because they'd have to pay taxes and list their addresses.

"The underground is available and receptive," Belforte said. "It has people who have been close to or involved with child theft or who have been hurt by the pro-mother bias of judges and laws. These fathers will buy whatever story a guy tells them and will give them room and board, watch their children, help them settle in somewhere.

"If you showed up at my office, or came to the bar, had your kid and wanted to hide, I'd assist you. If your wife called me, she'd be able, through me, to speak with your kids over the phone. But I wouldn't tell her where you are."

Belforte told of a man from Kansas City who came to him, claimed he had to steal his ten-year-old son. The man wound up in a rural town in New Mexico. "He called me after I sent him on to one of my contacts. The father became best buddies with the local magistrate, bought himself a little farm, began farming," Belforte said.

He protected that man and arranged for his ex-wife to speak with her stolen son.

"The mother called a couple of months later. She'd heard of me because of the magazine and asked if I'd spoken with him. I said, 'Yes, I know of your husband and where the boy is. They're doing fine.' She offered me any amount of money to tell, so she could get to them. I told her, 'No way.'

"I arranged for her to come to my office every Tuesday night at seven o'clock. She wanted to stay in El Paso for a month or two. She gave me cash for the phone. I would dial the number and she would talk to her son. The boy was happy to speak with his mother, but didn't want to say where he lived.

"The funny thing was, when she came to make her calls, she dressed up, lipstick and a dress. When she came over just to see me, she wore jeans. They talked like this for six weeks.

"Now, I have another recruit in that father. He trusts me, said I could put him on my list, that anytime I had someone in trouble, I should send him out to his place in New Mexico and he'd protect him," Belforte said.

6

The Mother's Perspective

Women, too, are angry at the laws and feel that child support orders can't be adequately enforced. They feel that men hide with their children to punish their former wives or to gain an advantage in court. However, women feel men steal children mainly for economic reasons.

Esther Jaoquine, a thirty-two-year-old librarian from Maryland, spoke for many mothers. Though at one point her husband, Roger, said she shouldn't have custody because she was a bad influence on their children, Esther feels her husband's motives for stealing their children were purely financial.

"It wasn't the courts," she said. "He didn't contest our divorce, didn't ask for custody. Yet he told me all along he wasn't going to give me a cent. Then the judge ordered him to pay two hundred dollars a month child support for our two children. My ex-husband sold insurance, but went back to his father's farm right after the court order came down."

Her ex-husband didn't pay child support for five months, and he didn't call or write his children. Then he just took them from where they lived with her in Bethesda, Maryland. It was on a weekend and they were playing outside. She didn't have the money to go to Nebraska.

"My lawyer wanted a thousand dollars," Jaoquine said.

"This was to fly to Omaha to file a writ of habeas corpus. My husband was at his father's farm near there. I didn't have any cash and didn't believe a midwestern judge would listen to me, much less pay attention to the Maryland court order."

Roger tried to bargain: She could have her children if she signed papers waiving child support, which she did. Two weeks later, in May 1979, she flew to Omaha, where her father-in-law met her at the airport. Her two children, a son, five, a daughter, three, ran to her.

"All he said was, 'Here they are,'" Jaoquine said. There wasn't any talk of Esther's fitness or goodness as a mother. "Just those three words, and then he left the airport. It was six hours before I got a flight to Chicago. We just waited near the check-in counter. I didn't want to go into town and wondered if I should hire a car and drive as far away as possible."

Esther Jaoquine picked up her life, unafraid because Roger could now keep his money. He hasn't bothered her since.

Her case is typical for mothers. Their ex-husbands give various excuses for stealing the children, usually saying laws are against them, individual judges don't like men, lawyers sell out fathers, or the mothers are unfit.

"Yet underneath there is money," said Marge Hopkins, a paralegal counselor with a women's center in Chicago. Hopkins, forty, has a bachelor's degree in social science from Northwestern University and was a caseworker with several county welfare departments in Illinois before joining the center. She married when she was twenty-three years old, has a fifteen-year-old son, was divorced from her first husband several years ago, and has since remarried.

She feels many mothers are vulnerable in divorce because they haven't worked outside the home and have had little experience with business and legal matters. "They don't think their children could be stolen," she said. "In fact, they really aren't prepared for the whole hassle—alimony, property settlements, custody. Women's centers like ours provide excellent counseling on financial and legal matters. But so far the women's movement hasn't addressed itself to child stealing."

Hopkins feels feminist leaders did well to gain equality for women—equal pay for equal work, recognition for careers as housewives—yet have been strictly concerned with property and money settlements in divorce. They take child custody for granted.

"Yet with divorce on the rise, fathers' rights, and now this seemingly growing problem of children being taken, I try to caution women to be careful about knowing where their husbands or ex-husbands live," she said.

Hopkins counsels women on all matters of divorce and has lists of lawyers they can hire once they leave her center. "It's especially important for women to know where they stand with the law. We don't want them taken advantage of by attorneys," she said. "Or, for that matter, taken advantage of by anyone. But lawyers are the first step in a divorce process. Perhaps the most important step, too."

She told of a mother who almost lost custody because of her own lawyer. He told the mother to move out of her home after the husband took their three children and went to Portland, Oregon. "The attorney told the woman to sign a paper giving her husband temporary custody of their children," Hopkins said.

It was bad advice for the mother, she pointed out. Courts might feel she abandoned the marriage by moving out. Also, they might give custody to her husband since he physically had the children.

"She'd given the attorney fifteen hundred dollars and there he was telling her she couldn't go back to her own home and she should give up custody," Hopkins said. "She'd moved in with her folks in a Chicago suburb and didn't know what to do. We found her a new attorney."

Cases like this lead women to distrust lawyers. They want to find someone they can speak to on their own terms. They know that sometimes male lawyers prey on female clients, and that there are lawyers who should not take divorce cases, but who do just the same because they think it might be easy money.

Many women counselors would agree with her, and they're making women more aware of child stealing besides just telling them how to fill out a budget when asking for alimony.

Women's groups and fathers' groups differ. Divorced women don't have much money, so finances are the main concern of their groups. Divorced men don't have custody, so children are one of their chief issues.

Women assume they'll have custody, and hope to have enough money and property to survive divorce. Men assume they'll *not* have custody and wonder how much of their salaries will go to women they no longer love. No one wins. Women feel they must fight for every penny and complain that working mothers aren't paid as much as working fathers. Feminist groups introduce and support bills on both federal and state levels to raise the economic standard of all women, but especially of career housewives. They talk about how much it would cost to hire someone to care for a home.

With so much attention on finances, women sometimes neglect child custody, and child stealing isn't one of their burning issues.

"It should be," said Louise Jacobs, a paralegal counselor with a women's center in Los Angeles. Married and with two children, Jacobs, thirty-nine, is a nurse by profession, but has a master's degree in counseling from the University of California at Berkeley, and has counseled about five hundred women in the past three years.

"Mothers take too much for granted about children," Jacobs said. "Sometimes I think they'd be better off giving them up to fathers and getting a career off the ground. It's why they broke up. They wanted to leave home and devote all their energies to their job.

"But women feel they *can't* give up their children. 'What would people say?' is a question mothers ask. They're stuck, and don't feel they can have both motherhood *and* a job.

"This angers fathers. Both sides accuse the other of wanting custody just for money. If the father has the kids, he doesn't pay, and he might avoid alimony, too, if his wife gets a job. And if the *mother* has them, she will receive child support and maybe alimony, too, because she can claim she has to stay home with her little ones."

Jacobs has seen parents start fighting over money, then argue over children. Both file for custody. If one parent feels scared, he or she might steal the children before a court decides.

"It's happened and it's going to happen again," Jacobs said. "They think of money and steal their children, tell the judge they should have custody and hope to win a better financial deal in their divorce.

"Fathers see it coming more than mothers, and are apt to take off first," she said. "This is why we counsel mothers on how to prevent a snatching, and we're trying to get feminists to take up the issue in state legislatures, along with their bills for enforcement of support."

Betty Remmart, twenty-eight, is a mother of three who went to Jacobs for help when her husband said he'd hired a lawyer and wanted to break up. "One of the first things I told Betty is to *always* know where her children are," Jacobs said.

She urged Remmart to get temporary custody as fast as she could. "But I didn't urge her soon enough," Jacobs explained. "Betty made the mistake of telling her husband she'd been to see me, and he stole their children a week later."

He held his children for ransom, made his wife a victim, too. "He said he wanted me to sign a separation agreement waiving all support money, now and in the future," Remmart said. "Yet he was willing for me to have the children."

Remmart couldn't find her husband and her children. His lawyer met with Jacobs and gave her all the papers. "He wouldn't say a thing about where his client lived," Jacobs said. "I told Betty to sign and found her a woman lawyer who felt the agreement could be overturned in court because Betty had signed under duress.

She signed. He returned the children. But as he left, Remmart had a process server give him papers ordering him to appear in court. Three months later a judge gave her custody and three hundred dollars in child support and alimony. Her husband deserted.

"She has her children, though," Jacobs said. "I've written other women's centers and told them Betty's story, told them to alert mothers about child stealing. If we hadn't acted quickly, we might have lost those children for good."

Jacobs has convinced some feminists to give child stealing a higher priority. "It's only part of a bigger problem," she said. "It's the worst kind of problem in divorce and makes divorce that much harder on women. They're victimized enough as it is and are emotionally and financially drained already without worrying about where their children are and who's feeding them."

Yet feminists seem to need a lot of convincing about the dangers of child stealing. One feminist explained how the National Organization for Women (NOW) works hard for economic rights for women, and described how children become drawn into money battles.

Lucille Kowan, fifty-eight, divorced, with two children, chairs NOW's New York State Task Force on Marriage and Divorce. Most of her work has been to get more money for divorced women.

NOW's main concern in New York, she said, has been to see that property is divided equally between husband and wife after they divorce. A bill to give courts power to divide money and property as they see fit became law in 1980. This law said property could be divided on an "equitable" basis, meaning judges could decide who got what and how much. NOW wants money and property divided on an equal, or fifty-fifty, basis, meaning judges have to split a family's assets down the middle.

She feels that under the existing system children can be drawn into money fights and that snatching, or the threat of it, may be used by a father to forge the kind of financial settlement he wants.

"In the early stages of divorce, most women tell me, 'I want my children to have a father,' " she said. "But the attitude changes as the money battle sets in. If the father has the ability to pay and doesn't, it pulls the children more and more into the situation. He might steal them to avoid paying support. But as the financial tension drops away, the children are used less and less. Even if the man doesn't pay, if the woman has a job and is secure, she is less frightened about losing her children. Also, the father is less likely to take them away."

Kowan said NOW doesn't favor joint custody. "We like joint custody as an option, not a mandate," she said. "I'm not in favor of it because it calls for a judge to use joint custody or else give reasons for *not* using it. If people are in the middle of a war, how can they share children?"

She feels, as do many others, that children should be given more attention in the courts. "I'd like to see the whole matter of custody pulled out of the courts to start with," she said. "I don't think courts are the proper place to settle matrimonial issues. Courts are too busy, too bored. They consider matrimonial problems the garbage pail of work and don't give it any kind of serious consideration. They don't uphold the truth. Perjury goes on all the time."

Kowan says NOW believes in equality, not just rights for women. "We're interested in women, but only to the extent that they get some kind of equality," she said. "Not to the extent that women get all the advantages and the tables are turned. That isn't our position. But I don't think that to gain some kind of equality, and have a better world for children, we should have divorces in courts. It becomes an adversary thing, with lawyers making a mint. They're the only real beneficiaries."

Child stealing and divorce are only secondary concerns of women's groups. It is achieving financial independence and equality that is their main concern.

Unfortunately, most feminists are either indifferent or hostile toward efforts to outlaw child stealing. No women's groups sent representatives to testify at the Congressional hearings in the spring of 1980. NOW hasn't taken a stand on S.105 and H.R.1290, and state and local feminist groups feel child stealing isn't a woman's issue. For the time being, at least, the problems of child custody and abuse will be relegated to a secondary position.

7

Legal Recourse

Child-stealing laws vary from state to state. But most states *do* treat child stealing as a crime provided a parent has been granted custody. If a custody order has not yet been handed down, most states treat child stealing as a family matter, and won't interfere.

Parents with custody have two methods of legal recourse —criminal and civil. The criminal way involves courts issuing and serving a felony or misdemeanor warrant for the arrest of the abducting parent, turning the children over to the victimized parent. The absconding parent may then be tried for interfering with a custody order.

In states that treat child stealing as a felony, a warrant for the arrest of the absconding parent can be sent to other states. If it's treated as a misdemeanor, the warrant is only good within the state. For most parents of stolen children, however, the problem is that even if they are able to obtain a warrant—whether felony or misdemeanor—they very rarely get help from authorities in tracking down their children.

If victimized parents are able to find the abductors on their own, then they may get help from the law. It happened to a woman in San Diego whose ex-husband took their sons to Oregon. She traced him through gasoline credit cards and had the felony warrant sent out. Police picked up her ex-husband, put the children in a shelter overnight and on a plane home the next day.

The civil method of recovering children costs more money, takes more time, and might not work. A parent of stolen children must hire an attorney and apply to a county or local criminal court for a writ of habeas corpus. A sheriff's deputy then serves the writ on the abducting parent, summoning him or her into court with the children. But the abducting parent might run before showing up in court. A writ of habeas corpus (which charges someone with legally detaining another person) with a writ of attachment (which authorizes legal authorities to recover the person) directs law enforcement authorities to pick up children when they serve papers on the abducting parent. The children are brought before a court, which then decides which parent should have them.

This civil method requires a victimized parent to hire an attorney and to spend money he or she might not have. Also, it can take a few days for the attorney to draw up the writ, have a judge sign it, and have law officials serve it on the abducting parent. By this time the parent might have moved, which happened to one father from Boston.

He found his four-year-old son and ex-wife on Long Island, hired an attorney, got his writ. But his ex-wife learned he was in town and left the state before the writ was served.

In other cases, though, writs of habeas corpus with writs of attachment have brought children into court and judges have given those children back to victimized parents who had custody.

This civil method depends on local judges. Since most stolen children are found in other states, it is always up to the judge in the new state to decide whether or not to honor custody papers from the home state. Some judges will; others won't. A mother from New York City brought her ex-husband and daughter into a Los Angeles court through these writs. A judge there honored her New York decree and gave back her child. Yet, a father from Cleveland brought his ex-wife and daughter into a Jackson, Mississippi, court and the judge refused to recognize his Ohio order. He gave the child to the ex-wife.

Regaining a stolen child sounds easy, and it *can* be, if the victimized parent has a valid custody order and if authorities in the new state where the child is uphold it. They won't help if there isn't a custody order and will probably ignore a noncustodial parent with a visitation order. Courts *may* tell an absconding parent who has custody to appear at some later date for a hearing on visitation, but by then he or she could have fled again.

The criminal approach—with a felony warrant—is best. It freezes the situation: The abductor is arrested, taken to police headquarters, posts bail. Police release children to the other parent.

This is why opponents of child stealing want a federal law making the offense a federal misdemeanor. Federal warrants can be served in any state.

But both civil and criminal approaches only *recover* children. They don't *find* them. And locating the children is 75 percent of the problem. Police may try to find an abductor if there is an arrest warrant, especially in states where it is a felony. But they use obvious methods. They ask questions of relatives and friends, who often deny everything. And then they stop investigating. They have no leads. There are other crimes to solve and they are overworked. They can't look out of state because they have no jurisdiction across state lines. Federal authorities, such as the FBI, can do that. But generally the bureau is reluctant and resists most attempts to find children. The FBI will look if several conditions exist: Local law enforcement authorities must obtain a felony warrant; the abductor must cross state lines; the children must be in physical danger; and the home county from which the children were abducted must be willing to extradite the alleged abductor. A federal attorney may then issue a federal warrant—for unauthorized flight to avoid prosecution (UFAP).

It can be hard to meet those requirements, though. What

if there is no felony warrant? Local district attorneys may not issue one because there may not be a custody order which was violated. Or law enforcement authorities might just be indifferent. Some take a wait-and-see approach. Maybe the abductor will voluntarily return the children within a few weeks. Maybe the situation isn't as bad as the hysterical, victim parent suggests.

The second and third requirements can be difficult to prove. What evidence is there that an absconding parent crossed state lines? Parents have been refused UFAP warrants because they couldn't prove where their former spouses went. What *is* proof? A letter from the abductor. But he or she hardly ever writes and says where the children are. Parents may claim they called long distance and spoke with their children and/or the abductor. Assistant district attorneys must decide if such "testimony" is proof. Some will, some won't.

How can a victimized parent prove his or her children are in danger? The absconding parent must have a history of instability, an irrational character that can be proved: alcoholism, brutality, violence, mental illness, child abuse. Law enforcement officials still want proof. Is there a police record of arrests for drunken driving, wife beating, disturbing the peace, creating a public nuisance? Was the abductor ever in a mental institution? Was there a complaint and investigation that he or she hit the children, bruised them, sent them to the doctor, the hospital?

What parents of stolen children allege about their spouses or former spouses is not enough. Husbands and wives always claim their partners are insane or brutal. Family squabbles are tough to solve, police say.

The Federal Parent Locator Service can help find children stolen in violation of a court order only. Victimized parents file complaints with police, who forward them to the district attorney. He will ask the state Parent Locator Service, which works with the Federal Parent Locator, to look

for absconding parents. However, only the most recent recorded address and place of employment of the parent will
be provided. Most absconding parents live with friends and
don't list true addresses with employers if they work.

These services will only *find* an abductor, not arrest him
or her or recover the children. They will notify the local
district attorney, who will decide whether to have the abductor arrested. It depends on what kind of warrant there is
in the home state.

Then, there is the problem of extradition, of sending home
an absconding parent with stolen children. Most states won't
extradite because it's too expensive, and other states won't
allow someone arrested in their state to be sent home. And
there is still the problem of having custody before the Parent
Locator Service will help. Most parents steal children before
there is a custody order.

"We've found that approximately eighty-five percent of
the time parents take off with kids before going to court,"
says Laurie Cancellara, head of the Stolen Children Information Exchange in California. And a Long Island group,
Children's Rights of New York, estimates that about 60
percent of its cases involve parents stealing children before
there are custody orders.

Even in states where laws theoretically help recover children, there's nothing built into them to prod law enforcement authorities to work. Federal and state officials take a
hands-off attitude toward domestic problems, especially
child stealing.

"Police don't want to get involved with family disputes,"
said Henry Foster, past chairman of the family law section
of the American Bar Association and an adviser in the draft-
ing of the Uniform Child Custody Jurisdiction Act and the
Uniform Marriage and Divorce Act. "Missing persons bu-
reaus stay clear of child snatching. Local and state prosecutors are uncooperative, and the Department of Justice and
FBI reject jurisdiction."

Foster pointed to how federal authorities *will* act in other areas, but ignore child abduction.

"It's ironic that there may be federal-state cooperation for the recovery of a stolen automobile or an adventurous female, but there is no cooperation for the return of a child," Foster said. "Perhaps our present public policy is more concerned about automobiles and sexual morality than it is about helpless children."

Foster feels Congress is wrong to cope with child beating, yet ignore child snatching. He also feels that parents themselves have contributed to this general laissez-faire attitude toward child stealing by constantly violating and ignoring custody and visitation orders. "With the exception of court orders for support, I know of no other area where court orders are violated with such frequency as those involving custody and visitation," he said. "Obviously, this leads to widespread disrespect for courts, lawyers, and the administration of justice in this country. It is a national disgrace that we have done so little to bring order out of chaos."

In a Senate hearing on new bills to make child stealing a federal crime, Foster explained how hard it was to recover children under the current laws. He told about one of his first child-stealing cases, where a "mother of two children had deserted her family and eloped to California with her boyfriend. The father, being apprehensive that the mother might return and spirit off the two children, got a court order awarding him legal custody.

"Nonetheless, the children were snatched and taken to California. We prepared extradition papers and sent them to the then governor of California, who steadfastly refused to cooperate. That governor later became a famous chief justice. The lesson I learned from that experience was that interstate cooperation in child-snatching cases was the exception rather than the rule."

Years later, a magazine editor wrote the American Bar Association about legal ethics. "The writer of the letter was the editor of *The Saturday Evening Post*," Foster said. "He reported that he had talked to a lawyer at a cocktail party in New York who told him that he was advising his client to use self-help in a custody dispute although such would be in violation of a court order.

"The editor wanted to know whether such advice was common, did it violate legal ethics, and what was being done about the problem.

"My letter in reply was a confession of guilt for the legal profession, the courts, law enforcement officials, and state legislatures.

"The lesson, as one justice put it, is that custody disputes are governed by a 'rule of seize and run, where possession apparently is not merely nine points of the law but all of them, and self-help the ultimate authority.' "

Foster once handled a case where a victimized parent pressed for damages. She sued her former in-laws for aiding and abetting in the child abduction, false imprisonment, and the intentional infliction of mental suffering. In this case, it was the *money*, not the custody issue, that brought the child home. His client was a mother in New York City whose son had been snatched by the father, with the help of his family, and then taken to Europe by the father. There was a bench warrant in Queens County for the abducting father's arrest.

"The sheriff for Queens told me that in order to have the warrant served I would have to inform him of the exact time and place for service and that I would have to get another warrant and use another sheriff for service outside of Queens."

"The attorney general, Department of State, Passport Control Office, members of Congress, et cetera, were informed of the facts, all to no avail," Foster said. "An attempt was made to have the father and his brother cited for contempt due to their deliberate obstruction of justice. The court refused. The United States attorney declined to consider prosecuting the father for depriving his son of his civil rights and his rights as an American citizen."

It was the money judgment that broke the case. The wife won a $181,000 judgment against her former father-in-law and former brother-in-law. "The family home in Queens was attached," Foster wrote. "The father-in-law and brother-in-law filed bankruptcy. They lost their business and were concerned about losing the family home." They convinced the husband to return the child, which he did.

Foster advises parents to go for a money judgment. "Courts should award damages against child abductors, and the person deprived of his legal right to custody should recover from the abductor the costs of locating and getting the child back."

There was a case, however, where Foster felt that snatching back a child was the only answer, despite legal means. A father took his sixteen-month-old daughter to Turkey in violation of a custody order. There was also a travel restriction written into the custody order which said he couldn't take his child out of the United States.

Foster learned that the courts would take eighteen months or longer to decide the case in Istanbul, and would probably rule in favor of the father, who was a Turkish citizen.

"For the first and only time I considered the alternative of snatching back the child, since an appeal to the Turkish court would be hopeless," he said. "Moreover, the Department of State, the Passport Control Office, and the Department of Justice refused to give us any direct aid or support, despite the intervention of three distinguished United States senators.

"The latter did all they could do, but were stonewalled by the federal bureaucracy," said Foster.

He and his client hired private investigators in England and learned the man had taken his daughter to Israel. Foster found the Israelis helpful.

"The father unwittingly had gone to one of the most co-operative countries in the world insofar as child custody matters are concerned," Foster said. "We knew we had him. Within a week the father was served with the equivalent of habeas corpus papers and was faced with civil and criminal court proceedings and the loss of his position as professor at a West Bank school for Arabs."

The man gave up his child when his ex-wife agreed to drop charges against him. But it cost the woman $30,000.

"Only custodians with access to substantial means can finance the expenses of retrieval," Foster noted, "and self-help in reverse is a costly and dangerous alternative that may be justified only as a last resort, when an appeal to the courts is hopeless."

8

The Legal Establishment

Parents find courts expensive and slow. Politicians who don't want snatching a federal crime say there are state laws to handle abduction. They point to uniform custody laws and say, "Find your former spouse, take him or her to court in a new state, have your home state custody order affirmed."

This is easier said than done, especially with the wait-and-see or hands-off attitude of public officials. But parents *do* track down abductors. They *do* haul them into court. But what then? Despite custody orders, arrest warrants, writs of habeas corpus, there is still a judge to deal with. What will that new judge do?

Children aren't given high priority in the legal system. Custody cases can pester judges. They aren't as exciting as rape, murder, or armed robbery. Some judges use the guideline of "home rule": Whoever lives in my county gets the children. They can do whatever they want and may claim they can decide custody even if other courts in different states have *already* decided it. One father from New York won custody of his daughter there, but his ex-wife fled to Kansas, where *she* won custody. She then moved to Phoenix, Arizona, and got custody again, in that state.

He spent over $25,000 dollars in both Kansas and then in Phoenix, trying to convince judges they should honor his New York order. But judges in those two new states demanded new hearings. Both parents hired lawyers.

The Kansas hearing lasted a day, with a judge saying that

the mother should have custody and that the New York order was not valid. The husband appealed, but his ex-wife left the state and hid for five months. When he found her again, in Phoenix, he took her to court there. This trial lasted three days. Again the judge ignored both New York's order and Kansas's order and gave custody to the mother because she said she lived in Arizona.

Parents can appeal a decision where a judge has ignored another custody order, but it can cost thousands of dollars more in legal fees and take many months before a new decision is handed down.

A father from Long Island learned the hard way about how judges can ignore uniform custody laws. He had custody of his son, yet was almost jailed for bringing him home.

Jack Tollen is a twenty-eight-year-old postal worker from Northport, New York. His seven-year-old son, Jack, Jr., of whom he had custody, was taken by Tollen's ex-wife in June 1979, after a normal weekend visit. Five months later Tollen found them in Miami, Florida.

But a Florida judge wouldn't recognize his New York order and said he could see his son for only two days before he had to return him to his ex-wife. Tollen, afraid his ex-wife would take off again, flew back to Long Island with his son instead. The Florida judge, angered by this, gave custody to Tollen's former wife without a hearing, and issued a felony warrant for Tollen's arrest. It is a felony in Florida to take a child out of state in violation of a custody order.

Others have had similar problems because judges can be inconsistent. Money judgments carry over from one state to another; custody decisions don't. A mother may be awarded child support in New York and have it upheld in Michigan. A bank or finance company may have a money judgment against someone in New Jersey and that judgment will be upheld in Illinois. Not so with custody of children, as parents keep finding out.

Harry Casson, a Los Angeles father, had custody of his

two sons, but his former wife abducted one of them, who was seven, to Ohio, in October 1976. Casson, thirty-six, an accountant, considers himself lucky to have his child back. But it cost him heavily, and he wonders if recovering the boy by vigilante methods might have been easier.

"I count myself extremely fortunate and blessed to have found my son within two months, but was hit by another blockbuster—a female juvenile judge who refused to honor my valid California custody decree and kept the matter in limbo for four and a half months," he said. "During this time she allowed the mother visitation rights in Ohio, even though she had been denied any visitation in California.

"On the other hand, I, who was awarded full custody about five years prior in the state of California, was not given *any* right of visitation and/or contact. . . . I finally was able to get my son back by suing the judge, together with the county officials and the children's care center in the city of Newark, Ohio, and brought suit at the court of appeals level. I was successful, the judge and county officials were found guilty of illegally detaining my son, and he was returned to my custody, some seven and a half months and twenty to twenty-five thousand dollars later."

Even though California had issued a felony warrant, Ohio didn't extradite his ex-wife. He said his former wife was not arrested and sent home to Los Angeles to stand trial because she had a sharp lawyer in Ohio and there was "some foot-dragging on the part of the governor's office in Sacramento, California. She could conceivably have gotten up to four years in jail under a very tough child-stealing bill that came into effect in the state of California as of January 1, 1977."

So parents who recover children through courts do so at great emotional and financial sacrifice. Jack Tollen spent $11,000 in Florida on lawyers alone. An Ohio father spent $40,000 and many months tracing his former wife through five western states.

Like Casson, Tollen wished he hadn't gone through the

courts, a view shared by many parents. He and his wife, Debra, separated in April 1975. She returned to live with him and their son a few months later, only to leave again in the summer. By January 1976, they were divorced. Debra threatened a long, expensive lawsuit if Tollen, who makes about $19,000 a year as a letter carrier, didn't give her custody. He agreed at the time. But the boy began living with Tollen and his new wife, Kathy, a twenty-four-year-old nurse, about a year after his divorce and remarriage.

"Debra would come, pick him up, keep him a couple of days and then return him," Kathy said. "She complained that he was too much for her to handle. She lived in Brooklyn and would come out and see Jackie in Northport about every other weekend."

Kathy grew fond of little Jack. "I've been raising him from the time he was three," she said. "Before we were married the boy spent most of his time with my husband's mother and whenever it was possible, we had him here. Jack has to leave for work at six o'clock in the morning and there was no way he was going to get Jackie out of bed and take him over to his mother's at that time. Jackie had his own room at his grandmother's house and just about every night we were over there for supper. When I moved in, we kept the boy with us."

Debra had other ideas in the fall of 1978. She came to visit her son one November afternoon and said to Tollen she was keeping the boy. For good. She still had legal custody, even though she was a runaway mother.

"She sent Jackie out to the car with her boyfriend," Tollen said, "and told me she wanted to talk and that's when she told me to forget it, she wasn't going to bring him back. She had the custody papers with her."

Tollen went outside and saw the car window rolled down. He leaned in to grab his son and the car started moving. He held on to the door as Debra and her boyfriend started away with Jackie between them.

"My feet dragged along the ground and I could feel the wheels kicking at the soles of my feet," Tollen said. One of his neighbors called the police as he was being dragged along. Finally the car stopped, but when the police came they read Debra's papers and told her to take the child away.

Tollen sued for custody a week later. The New York State supreme court gave him temporary custody and, after several postponements, gave him permanent custody of the boy in June 1979.

"Then I told her we had to sit down and work out visitation," Tollen said. "We had an agreement with our lawyers that she would have Jackie for the weekend of June 29, and when she brought him home, we'd meet and work out these details."

They never met.

Debra took the child, but soon called to say she wouldn't show up again. Ever.

Kathy Tollen told what it was like during that summer, especially as a stepparent. "I worked at a day camp taking care of little kids," she said. "That was hard, but it was bittersweet, too. All these maternal instincts I had for Jackie during those years would come out when some little child about his age with a banged up head from being hit by a ball would come to me. I kept wondering if Jackie was going through any of the same things.

"It was very hard, working with kids the same age every day and not knowing where Jackie was," she said.

Yet it kept her, and Jack Tollen, going. "It seemed important that I be around other children," Kathy said. "A lot of that was a fire that kept us going. We'd see kids from broken homes and kids from rich parents and we'd see what happens to these kids because of the way they've been brought up. It became more important that Jackie be found and brought up with us."

In the fall they traced Debra to Miami through credit cards she'd used to buy gas down the East Coast. The Tollens' lawyer subpoenaed the oil company and they gave him her receipts. They knew she was in Miami now, but *where* in Miami?

"We triangulated an area through a layaway plan she had with one of the stores," Kathy said. Jack Tollen then went into one of the elementary schools and asked for his son. He was lucky. One of the secretaries had once lost *her* children this way and told him to call a central office in Dade County which would tell him where Jackie was. From that central office Tollen learned which district his son was in. He also learned where he lived.

But it wasn't over.

Tollen had his custody papers from New York and decided taking his son as he came out from school might be scary. He decided to have the sheriff pick up the child on a writ of habeas corpus and take him into court.

He now thinks that was a mistake.

"Florida has this law which says a judge can take jurisdiction over an out-of-state custody case if he thinks it is in the best interest of the child," Tollen said.

Jackie came into court on Friday, December 7, 1979. "The judge flip-flopped back and forth," Tollen said. "First he said, 'I'm not going to change this man's custody. I'm not going to change custody of another state.' Then he decided to question me, and said we should see a psychiatrist. Finally, he said I could visit with Jackie for the weekend and should return him to Debra Sunday night. How could I do that? She might vanish again."

Tollen and Jackie took a plane for New York that night. Two days later the judge gave custody to Debra and issued a felony warrant for Tollen's arrest. It meant that warrant could be sent to New York and Tollen arrested for violating a Florida custody order. It also meant that Debra wouldn't be punished for violating a *New York* custody order as long as she didn't return to Long Island.

He hired a Florida lawyer who wanted $7,500 right away. Tollen had time against him. His lawyer in Florida said as soon as he got the money he'd move to have the state's attorney in Florida keep the warrant. He also said the judge had a good reputation, was a friend of one of his law partners, and he would see what he could do.

But he needed his money. If he didn't get it soon, he might not be able to stop that warrant from being sent up, he said. Tollen thought of going into hiding, but he had a good job and so did Kathy. They thought Jackie had been moved around too much.

Their money held the warrant and got a conference with the judge, who dropped the warrant after Tollen returned, without his son. "I went down on a night flight," Tollen said. "I was scared. There was still a live felony warrant for me. I could have been put in jail. The judge agreed to drop it, but he still wouldn't change his order giving custody to Debra."

Tollen had to come up with another $3,500 to appeal, and finally won his case.

Jack Tollen was lucky in the end: He recovered his son *despite* the court system today. Many other parents and children run afoul of that system, though. A Baltimore attorney, Archibald Eccleston, told of a South Dakota mother who fought red tape, like Tollen, only she didn't recover her son. "Her child, a boy of eight years of age, was spending a regular two-day visit with his father, which started on May 25, 1979, and ended on May 27, 1979. On May 28, 1979, when the child was not returned, his mother frantically contacted relatives of her ex-husband in Nevada, California, and Colorado.

"They had not heard from her ex-husband at that time.

"On further investigation, she found that he had quit his job, moved from his apartment, and canceled his phone service—all on May 25, 1979, the day he left with their son. On May 29 the mother contacted her attorney to determine what steps could be taken. She was informed by her attorney that he could not be of any assistance and that she must solicit the assistance of the state authorities.

"She then proceeded to contact the state's attorney's office where she was advised that they would 'look into it.' They gave her very little encouragement, stating that it was strictly a civil case.

"On June 5, 1979, she filed a missing person report with the sheriff's office and with the police department. She also filed reports with the Department of Social Services and Child Custody Agency. In early June, on her own, she sent change-of-address cards to her ex-husband's creditors, hoping she might trace his whereabouts in that fashion. She did finally trace her ex-husband as far as Utah and forwarded that information to the state's attorney in South Dakota.

"On June 27, she wrote the governor and was informed that this matter was not under his authority. The governor forwarded a copy of her letter to the state attorney general. A letter from the attorney general advised her that he, too, was unable to help, and he forwarded a copy of her letter to the county state's attorney.

"The mother then contacted her U.S. senator, who informed her that his staff had contacted both the FBI and the South Dakota Division of Criminal Investigation. On July 19, she again contacted the state's attorney to inquire what could be done.

"He suggested that she contact her local state senator regarding state legislation. She was then advised by an attorney of a South Dakota law that had been passed on July 1, 1979, regarding child snatching, but was told that the law did not apply to her since it was passed on July 1, 1979, and her son was taken on May 25, 1979.

"In addition, because the law was applicable only in situations involving noncustodial parents who take or entice away their unmarried minor children from the custodial parent without prior consent, she was advised that it would not apply to her case because her ex-husband merely failed to return the child after prior consent," Eccleston said.

This "taking and enticing away" problem is the same in New York State as in South Dakota. New York parents sometimes cannot get misdemeanor warrants on abducting parents because of it. Judges and district attorneys in the Empire State have used that loophole in the state's custodial interference law to turn down a parent who wants police and court help. If a parent takes a child under normal visitation, as outlined by a court order, he or she is not "taking or enticing away from custody."

Eccleston continued, "On August 17, the distraught mother, on her own, contacted the schools in the area in the belief that they might have received requests for her son's school records from other schools. She contacted her son's doctor in the event that his health records had been requested. She contacted the Register of Deeds in Rapid City and Pierre in the event they received requests for her son's birth certificate, believing that these might be required if her son were enrolled in a new school.

"On August 21, 1979, again on her own, she completed and mailed 483 reward posters offering a thousand dollars for information regarding her son. She sent these to people involved in her ex-husband's usual occupation, elementary schools, unions, state departments of education, sheriff's offices and police departments in all areas where her ex-husband had relatives.

"On August 28, 1979, the Las Vegas Police Department contacted the Rapid City, South Dakota, Police Department and the Pennington County Sheriff's Office to determine if there was a warrant issued for the ex-husband. They had received a poster from a school and were investigating. When they were informed by the sheriff that there was not a warrant issued, they advised that there was nothing they could do. Her local state's attorney told her he would 'continue checking into the matter.'

"On August 29, she received a telephone call from a woman who worked in Las Vegas with her ex-husband, and who was interested in the reward. The mother once again contacted the sheriff's office and the state's attorney's office for help. She was informed that nothing could be done and it was up to her to 'steal' her son back. The following morning the mother and her brother flew to Las Vegas, only to learn that her ex-husband had seen a poster that day and had left the area, possibly for California.

"On September 4, 1979, she contacted a judge in South Dakota and asked that a warrant be issued for her ex-husband for contempt of court on the basis that her ex-husband had been enjoined prior to the May 25 visitation from removing the child from the state of South Dakota. The judge advised her that because her ex-husband was out of the state he could only issue an 'immediate custody order.'

"On September 5, 1979, the mother prepared and mailed an additional 250 posters to California. On September 18, 1979, a call was received from a woman in California who advised the mother that her ex-husband had been staying with her, was carrying a gun, and using hard drugs.

"She was advised that her son was 'emotionally disturbed and neglected, totally withdrawn, would not play with other children, and sits and stares as though he is hollow.' The mother again contacted all of the authorities, the state's attorney, the sheriff, the police department, the Department of Social Services and the FBI as well as the local judge. Again, she received the same answers: 'Sorry, there is nothing we can do.'

"I quote for you the last paragraph of that mother's letter:

The anger and frustration from being bounced around and told SORRY over and over again are nothing compared to the very real pain, anguish, and torment that I feel without my son. It is an agony that is tearing me to pieces. I have obtained another 500 posters and I will start again. Someday, somewhere I am going to find my son and have him home again. I will never quit. I have had to work two jobs for the past three months to pay for attorney's fees, posters, and wasted trips out of state.

Perhaps by keeping so completely busy I might just keep from going insane. Thanks for listening to my story. I cannot truly understand that any human being should have to go through such a nightmare when proper legislation could serve to curb and correct child snatching."

9

The Laws:
The Worst and the Best

Until child stealing becomes a federal crime, all fifty states can deal with it any way they like. All counties can deal with it any way they like, too. And all judges can deal with it as they see fit, also.

They can ignore uniform custody or uphold it. Honor another state's custody or reverse it. Order a new trial or send parents back to their home states. Punish child stealers or let them go. Order lawyers for abductors to reveal where their clients hide or try cases without those abductors present.

Some judges enforce custody or visitation, others don't. Most feel money is more important than children. They'll enforce support, but not the rights of children to see both parents. Most ignore child stealing, won't issue warrants or punish an abductor if he or she is brought home. Only a handful of abductors go to jail. Barely a handful more pay fines. They must return to their home states to stand trial if they violated a custody order. But usually they don't return, and most states won't extradite.

As mentioned before, child-stealing laws vary widely in strength and enforcement. They range, across the country, from very weak—in which grounds for legal interference are almost impossible to obtain—to quite strict—where child stealing can be treated as a federal crime, both in the laws themselves (with a federal "unlawful flight to avoid prosecution" warrant) *and* by the legal establishment that enforces them. New York is an example of the worst it can be; California represents the best.

In New York, parents have trouble getting police or district attorneys to help, even if they have custody. And judges will look for loopholes in New York's law to avoid issuing criminal warrants. Child stealing is a misdemeanor in New York *only* if the abductor "takes or entices away" a child from someone who has lawful custody. This means that if parents visit their children on weekends, according to a court order, and don't return them, they may not have committed a crime: They didn't "take or entice away" children. They just didn't return them.

If, however, they broke into homes, stole the children out of their beds at night and during times when there wasn't court-ordered visitation, then they *might* be charged with custodial interference. But they *might not* be, also.

A mother once came for her six-year-old daughter on New Year's Eve. It was ten thirty at night, and raining. The father was out and a baby-sitter answered the door. The mother wrapped her sleeping child in a blanket, and drove off into the storm. It was a Wednesday night. Her days for visitation were Friday night until Sunday night, with twenty-four hours' notice. She didn't give notice, though, didn't call the father ahead of time and ask to visit with her child.

He couldn't get an arrest warrant. He took his court order and a copy of the New York State Penal Code to precinct headquarters, but it didn't work. Luckily, the mother returned their daughter several days later. The father didn't sleep well for a month after that.

New York's law enforcement authorities often contend that child stealing is a family dispute and should be settled civilly, with court delays and expensive lawyers. They'll point to the law and use it as an excuse *not* to investigate.

"It's only a misdemeanor, a minor crime," they'll say. There are many unsolved felonies they must work on.

The New York State Assembly's Codes Committee has tabled a bill to make child snatching a felony since 1977. Yet there are thirty *other* states that treat the problem as a felony. Alaska has better anti–child stealing laws than New York, for instance. So do Arkansas, Colorado, Connecticut, Georgia, Iowa, Kansas, Louisiana, Missouri, to name a few. Oklahoma calls parental kidnapping child stealing and lists it under the state's kidnapping statutes as a felony. West Virginia calls it child snatching, but also lists it as a felony under its kidnapping statutes, as does Wyoming, which calls it child stealing and makes it a felony.

A handful of the many cases in New York stand out as examples of how poorly this problem is handled. All show the reluctance of that state's officials to help.

A Long Island woman lost her two girls, ages five and two, when her ex-husband took them for a weekend visit in December 1979. Donna Gaines, thirty, thought he might be with his family in Arkansas when he didn't bring them home by Sunday night.

She had custody of the girls and worked as a paralegal counselor with a public legal services corporation. A graduate of Southampton College on Long Island, she tried to use the law, but couldn't.

"They wouldn't give me a misdemeanor warrant in Suffolk County," she said. "My lawyer and I talked with an assistant district attorney and a judge, but they wouldn't put out a warrant on him."

She had that problem of "taking or enticing away" in New York's misdemeanor law, and public officials who were quick to find that loophole.

"One judge told me, 'If you can convince me on the law that I should sign this warrant, I'll sign,'" Gaines said. "He told me, 'Your husband took his children on his regular visitation. That's not enticement.' People who interpret this law have never been through this kind of situation," she said. "If my husband had taken them on a day when he wasn't supposed to, or had forced his way into the house, that would have been different. I was angry, furious."

She finally located them in Texas, where the police were considerably more helpful. She's since returned to Long Island with her children, but hasn't been able to press charges against her husband because the judge never signed the warrant after he had stolen her children. She's afraid he might take them again, since he wasn't punished.

That "taking and enticing" loophole in New York's law also worked against a father and his five-year-old daughter. His story also tells something about New York's politics, judges, and lawyers, which both feminists and fathers' rights groups agree need changing.

The father, Ronald LaMora, a thirty-two-year-old machinist in Sayville, New York, and his wife, Betty, twenty-five, separated in August 1977. They had lived with their daughter, Melissa, in Sayville until Betty went into a local hospital because of emotional problems. She was depressed and had tried to kill herself.

When she came out of the hospital two months later, she went to live with her parents in North Bellmore, which is in Nassau County on Long Island. Sayville is in Suffolk County. Betty continued outpatient therapy at a second hospital.

During this time Melissa stayed with her father, who was given temporary custody of her in November 1977. A second judge continued the temporary custody when the couple divorced in June 1978.

In the fall of 1978 the couple went to family court in Suffolk County to argue permanent custody. The county's Department of Health Services recommended the girl stay with her father. Both parent and child had lived together, without the mother, in the family home for a year. The child went to school in the same district where she'd grown up. The mother lived with her parents part of the time and in an apartment of her own some of the time. However, the judge gave custody to the mother.

She then vanished with Melissa.

LaMora claims his ex-wife's lawyers wouldn't tell where his daughter was. He pestered police until they issued a misdemeanor warrant. She surrendered after six weeks, posted bail, and was released. At her trial some time later, a criminal court judge and an assistant district attorney dropped the charges against her because she didn't "take or entice away" the child.

Ron LaMora appealed the custody decision to the appellate division of the state supreme court.

The judges made note of the girl's abduction and concealment in their decision. They wrote, "We condemn such conduct as utterly unbecoming of a parent concerned with the best interests of the child and as in apparent contempt of the order which we uphold today . . . we decline to offer even faint approval of the mother's behavior. . . ." But the final decision of the court was to leave custody with the mother.

There were two other cases where Long Island parents had trouble getting law enforcement authorities to enforce custody orders. And a third case had a family court judge in Suffolk County sending police and sheriff's deputies after a sixteen-year-old boy who wanted to live with his father instead of with his mother.

In the first case, a Queens mother sued the Suffolk County sheriff for not picking up her eighteen-month-old son, who'd been stolen by her ex-husband in August 1978. She'd hired a lawyer and an investigator, and in December 1978 learned where her son was. When she asked the sheriff to recover him, the sheriff refused. He claimed she didn't pay a twenty-dollar matron's fee to have a woman go with the deputies to get the boy. She paid the matron's fee in January 1979.

Deputies went to a home where the ex-husband and boy had been. But they were gone.

"I could have had my little boy home except for the laziness of the sheriff's office," the woman said.

The sheriff said he could have been held liable if he sent deputies to pick up the child without a matron. Why didn't he just recover the boy and collect the fee later? It wasn't the right procedure, one of his aides said.

In a second case, a Long Island mother who had custody of her two-year-old daughter claimed she told police where her ex-husband was but they wouldn't go to the house and recover her baby.

Violet Lutz, twenty-three, last saw her two-year-old daughter in November 1978. The couple had divorced in June 1978, after a three-year marriage, with custody going to her and weekend visitation to her ex-husband. But on one of his weekend visits, her ex-husband, Allan, twenty-eight, stole their child. In July 1979, she tracked Allan to the home of his mother in Islip, on Long Island. She took copies of her custody papers and sat in a car near the house, waiting for Allan to show up on their daughter's birthday.

She saw her ex-husband and their daughter drive up to his mother's home and walk inside. Her first impulse was to run after them and try to grab her baby. Instead, she called police.

They didn't respond.

"There were other people inside the home," an officer said. "There was an infant in there, too, who could have been injured in a fight."

He admitted there might have been another reason for police not to help.

"You don't have to look at the divorce rate among police officers to know there are mixed emotions about domestic situations," he said.

"We came so close," Violet said. "I don't even remember driving away. That night I kept screaming, 'I don't believe it, I don't believe it.' There was my baby. She'd been kidnapped and I should have broken down the door and kidnapped her back."

Now she has lost track of her husband, her one opportunity wasted. The Suffolk County police say they don't have enough men to help her find her child again. So, alone, she is still looking.

Politicians and police in New York State admit there is a men's rights backlash against efforts to stop child stealing. Legislators drag their feet on enacting stronger laws, and law enforcement authorities drag theirs on enforcing weak ones. "Most of the politicians are men," said Jonathan Stern, a research assistant to a New York City assemblyman. "They feel child stealing isn't something they should mess with. Also, in most divorces, custody of children is given to the mother. Some of these guys feel they should have the right to snatch their kids."

Police, who don't like family disputes anyway, have similar feelings. "It might be one of us someday who leaves with his kid," said one Suffolk County patrolman. He echoed the unofficial policy of most law enforcement officials in the Empire State. "When we find that it's a parent who's left with the kid, then it becomes a family dispute or custody fight and we get out of it fast," he said.

One Suffolk County family court judge, on Long Island, *did* enforce another state's custody once, *did* search for a child, *did* threaten both a father *and* son with jail if they disobeyed him.

But it was for the wrong reason.

It started in November 1975, when Timothy Schafner, forty, and his first wife, Elinor, thirty-nine, divorced in New York. She got custody. Three days after their hearing Schafner went to visit his son, Timmie, in Dix Hills. He took his new girlfriend, Kim, with him.

"We went to the door," Schafner said, "and a woman answered. She said Elinor didn't live there anymore. She didn't know where my ex-wife and son were. She rented the home from Elinor's attorney.

"I asked where she mailed the rent and she told us to a post office box," he said.

The woman gave Schafner an oil painting of Timmie. There was a note on it: "This is the last you'll see of your son."

Timothy and Kim went to police, Elinor's attorney, a family court judge, but no one would help them find Timmie. Schafner wrote letters to a post office box which Elinor's attorney had given him, and didn't send her money. He soon married Kim and still wrote letters and cards to that post office box throughout 1975 and during most of 1976.

Schafner, who worked as a mechanic in a fabric factory which Kim owned, felt his first wife might be in Florida, since she'd often said she liked Miami or Fort Lauderdale. She had a son from an earlier marriage and liked military schools.

That was their clue.

Kim flew to Florida and checked military academies. She learned Timmie was in such a school in Fort Lauderdale by calling the superintendent of schools. He wouldn't give the boy's home address, though.

Timothy asked a family court judge in New York to force the schools' superintendent to reveal where Timmie lived, but the judge refused. He simply told Timothy to send his child support to that post office box. "We don't look for children," the judge said. "Only for parents who owe money."

Schafner's attorney then wrote the military school, and was given Timmie's address when he threatened to sue them for false imprisonment. This was in November 1976, and Schafner began to send letters to this new address.

There were still no replies.

Timothy Schafner went to family court again and asked to legally suspend Elinor's child support. She was in contempt for not letting him see his boy, he claimed. The court turned him down, saying the boy needed to be supported even if his father couldn't see him.

He couldn't wait any longer. One Thursday night in April 1977, Timothy and Kim Schafner got on an Eastern Airlines flight at La Guardia Airport and went to Florida.

The Schafners waited in a rented car near Elinor's house the next morning. Timmie came out and went to a bus stop. They drove up and rolled down the window. Timmie didn't recognize them and turned away. His father got out and went to him, and Timmie realized who he was and started to cry. They hugged each other. It had been a long year and a half.

His father and Kim asked Timmie if he wanted to come to New York for the weekend. He said he did, but wanted to call his mother first. Timothy was cautious. He knew his ex-wife. They went to the airport first, booked a flight, waited until it was time to get on.

Then Timmie called his mother.

They saw police cars drive to the passenger terminal as their plane lifted off.

New York police waited for them, but in the baggage area. All the Schafners had was hand luggage. They left the airport without being seen and, once home, called Elinor to say Timmie would come back Sunday night.

She was furious. The next day, Saturday, police came to Timothy and Kim's house with Elinor's custody order, a new order Timothy Schafner hadn't seen. It was from Florida and they said New York recognized it.

But when he read it, he realized it gave him visitation. The police ignored his protests, though, and brushing him aside, they took Timmie. Schafner went to his attorney, who drew up a writ of habeas corpus. They served it on Elinor before she left New York, and she came back two weeks later because of it. Finally, Timothy Schafner got help. A Suffolk County judge told Elinor she *had* to send Timmie to his father for eight weeks in the summer of 1977 or he would send an order to Florida for a sheriff to put Timmie on a plane and her in jail.

Timmie flew north for July and August that summer. The boy wanted another week in Port Jefferson. Elinor told him, "No," that he should take a good look at his father because it would be his last look.

The boy went back to Florida, but called several weeks later: He wanted to move, said his mother screamed at him. Schafner sent him twenty dollars and bought a plane ticket. Timmie just had to pick it up at the airport. The boy packed his clothes while his mother and her new husband were at work.

However, a neighbor saw him get into a taxi and called Elinor, who sold real estate. Police met Timmie at the airport and took him to their station, where Elinor came to pick him up.

Timmie didn't come up for the summer of 1978. He never called his father. Elinor changed their phone number in Fort Lauderdale again.

Timothy Schafner ran into more trouble in New York. A family court judge ordered him to pay child support, said he'd hold him in contempt if he didn't pay the *back* child support, which they call arrears. Timothy hadn't paid anything since the beginning of July 1978, when Elinor violated the visitation order. He told the judge he couldn't see his son; eight weeks in two years wasn't fair. But the judge refused to enforce his visitation order, saying it wasn't that important, the boy had one parent, at least, and lived in a different state. Florida was too far away to have the visitation enforced, he felt.

Schafner had to pay. Only if the boy didn't come up for the summer of 1979 would the court consider suspending child support.

Schafner and his wife mailed certified letters to Elinor. She didn't pick them up. They went to court again on June

22, 1979, told that same judge they hadn't heard anything. He said, "Mail more letters," which they did. The judge felt Schafner should keep trying to contact his son through the mail and not do anything else.

On Friday, June 29, Timothy went to the dentist. Elinor called his home and told Kim that Timmie would be on a flight that day, arriving at five o'clock. They drove to the airport not knowing what to think, but the boy was there.

He hugged his father and said he'd run away fifteen times during the school year. Once he'd been gone two weeks.

"Why did she send you, then?" his father asked.

"She was tired of the hassle," his son told him.

Schafner was able to get temporary custody of Timmie in the summer of 1979. It was from a state supreme court judge. But Elinor was on the warpath again. She came to New York, went to the family court judge who'd handled the case before, and he overturned the supreme court order, saying Timmie should return immediately to Florida, despite the fact that the supreme court in New York is a higher court than family court. Normally, judges in lower courts don't overturn decisions from higher courts.

Elinor and the police came to Schafner's home again, but Timmie had run away. No one could find him. They searched the neighborhood, but the boy wasn't around, so Elinor left. Schafner got a stay on the family court order returning custody to his ex-wife.

But in February 1980, the appellate division turned down his appeal: Timmie would have to go back to Florida.

The family court judge was angry that Schafner had tried to overturn his order. The judge said Florida had jurisdiction because of Elinor's new order. Everyone should abide by it, and Timothy had better pay his arrears and resume child support or go to jail.

It was Thursday, March 13, 1980, in Hauppauge, New York. The judge wouldn't listen to Timmie, who was two months away from his sixteenth birthday. Timmie ran from the courtroom, from the building, into hiding. He'd been in school in Port Jefferson, but now couldn't go to class. He'd had a home, but couldn't go to it.

His stepfather, who'd come to take him back, claimed it was planned, a setup. The judge issued an arrest warrant. Police and sheriff's deputies searched areas near Schafner's home, went to Timmie's school, questioned his friends.

"I just decided that if they are going to send me back, then I'm going to take off," Timmie said. He felt time was on his side and he would hang out until his birthday. No one knew where he was going to run or where he was.

"While I'm with my mother, I get violent sometimes," he said. "She plays weird games with my head." Elinor told people her son was brainwashed. "He doesn't know himself," she said.

Kim Schafner's factory was in East Islip, New York. They had told Timmie to go there when he ran away. But he went to a store and called them at home. They picked him up in a delicatessen in Smithtown and drove to the factory that evening. What should they do? They found a friend in Centereach who took him in. Then they found a Catholic priest who let Timmie stay in his rectory.

He was inside all day, every day, and took walks at night. After two months, when he was sixteen, he got a job in a nursery in Mount Sinai, a few miles from Port Jefferson.

Every day for weeks police and deputies came to the Schafner house. The judge was mad, they said, really mad. First, Timothy didn't pay support. Then, the boy ran. Timothy and Kim said over and over they didn't know where the boy was. Officers searched their home, attic, basement, garage, went to neighbors. Elinor came from Florida. *She* searched their home, too.

"We just couldn't believe they wanted to arrest him," Kim said. "But we were willing to stick it out. If the warrant wasn't dropped, we'd try to have his schoolwork brought home to us."

Timmie Schafner turned sixteen the second week of May 1980. The priest got him a lawyer and they tried to have the boy emancipated, which meant he was on his own, self-supporting, had a place to live. He came out of hiding and went into court. A *Newsday* reporter was there. The judge, seeing the reporter and the priest, had second thoughts. There had been one article in *Newsday* already about Timmie's running away from the courtroom. He ordered the boy to stay at the parish rectory and return in seven days to decide the emancipation.

"We lost the battle, but won the war," Kim Schafner said a week later. The judge denied the emancipation, but said he wouldn't issue another warrant. He dropped the first one and told Timmie to go back with his stepfather and mother, who'd come up from Fort Lauderdale again.

"A court officer took him to their car, but whispered to Timmie, 'Wait until my back is turned before you do anything.' Timmie looked at his mother and said, 'See you around, Mom.'"

He went to his father and Kim, who drove off quickly. Elinor ran into the courtroom, looking for police, screaming. There were no officers around, and she left that afternoon for Florida.

"I'm feeling really great," Timmie said several days later. "I'm living at home in Port Jefferson, where I belong. My mother might come over with the police and try to get me, but I'll just show them my birth certificate. I have to settle back into school and want to keep my job. The lawyer said they can't do anything. No law is broken. At sixteen, I can live where I want."

While New York may have weak laws and indifferent officials to enforce them, California has one of the best state laws dealing with child stealing and some of the most cooperative district attorneys and police, officials sensitive to the problem.

Parents from other states usually have little trouble recovering stolen children from California *if* they have custody orders and know where their children are. There have been many cases where parents have gone to law enforcement authorities in California with certified copies of their home state's custody papers and found police and other officials willing to go out and retrieve the children.

In Los Angeles there have been two public hearings on both federal and state laws regarding child stealing. One was in March 1977, about a proposed new California law, now in effect; another was in April 1979, about the two federal bills, S.105 and H.R.1290, which were considered in Congress.

Both senators from California have co-sponsored the Wallop bill, to make snatching a federal crime, and one of them, Alan Cranston, chaired the 1979 hearing on it. California is one of few states that regards child stealing as an offense by itself, and can serve as a model for other states.

Dr. Michael Agopian, thirty-three, professor of criminal justice at California Lutheran College in Thousand Oaks, California, spent three years studying how police and sheriff's deputies treated child stealing in Los Angeles County. California passed a law in July 1977 that gave district attorneys the choice of treating child snatching as a misdemeanor or a felony, and judges the option of putting parents in jail for one, two, three, or four years, fining them $10,000, or both, as a felony, or putting them away for a year, fining them $1,000, or both, as a misdemeanor.

Agopian pointed out that the original law read that a person had to "maliciously take, entice away, detain or conceal a minor child" in order to be charged with a crime in California. It was hard to prove someone was "malicious" in taking children, much as it is still hard to prove someone "took or enticed" a child in New York.

The old California law also said a person had to snatch the child in the state and had to do so "without good cause," Agopian said.

"Now, you only have to show that a parent or relative detained or concealed a child, no matter where the abduction or concealment took place," he said. "The new law also enforces a parent's visitation rights and makes it a crime to refuse visitation that is in the custody decree. And 'good cause' is no longer a defense. The offending parent's motives don't matter."

Most important, the new California law—Penal Code Section 278—gives district attorneys the power to use all state, county, and local agencies to find missing parents and stolen children.

Agopian pointed out there were flaws, though. The new law won't work if there isn't a custody order; it doesn't help a noncustodial parent to visit with children if the custodial parent moves to another state; and it doesn't work if a couple wasn't married when they had children.

Agopian's study of child stealing in Los Angeles County examined ninety-one criminal cases closely. He found that fathers stole children twice as much as mothers in those cases. "Males were the offender in seventy-one percent of the crimes, while females accounted for twenty-nine percent of the offenses," he said. "It must be recognized that child stealers are overwhelmingly males because custody awards almost always favor mothers as the custodial parent."

Agopian learned that both abductors and victimized parents were "generally young and within the same age group. Most offenders, thirty-five percent, and most victimized parents, also thirty-five percent, were between twenty-seven and thirty-one years of age," he said. "And seventy-three percent of the offenders and seventy-six percent of the parental victims were thirty-six years old or younger. The mean age of offenders was thirty-six years and the mean age of victimized parents was thirty-three years."

Agopian found that child stealing is a low-risk crime, even in a state such as California, where laws against it are tough. Of the ninety-one cases considered for prosecution by the

Los Angeles County district attorney's office between July 1, 1977 and June 30, 1978, after California's new law went into effect, criminal charges were filed in only fifty.

The first step the district attorney took in those cases was to see if a custody order was violated. If there was no custody order, or there was one but it was vague, criminal action might not be taken. "The initial desire is to settle the matter without creating a criminal action," he said. "The district attorney's office might send a letter to the offending parent informing him or her of the law and the possibility of a criminal charge," Agopian said. "Also, the use of mediation in the form of an office conference may be sufficient in rectifying the case.

"The second policy step is to initiate a misdemeanor prosecution," he explained. "The final course is a felony charge. Felony prosecutions are utilized in aggravated cases that might include a history of prior thefts, elaborate schemes, or the disappearance of the parent or child. If a child's whereabouts is unknown or the child is believed to be in another jurisdiction, a felony charge is appropriate in order to invoke extradition proceedings."

Forty-one of the cases Agopian studied were dismissed. Agopian said thirteen were because of incomplete evidence and another thirteen were referred to the city attorney for possible misdemeanor charges. Charges were dismissed in the interest of justice in eight cases. The remainder were dismissed for miscellaneous reasons.

"The prosecution of parental child-stealing offenses is limited primarily by the failure of information to link the suspect with the crime, locating the offending parent, or the desire to resolve such matters without criminal action," Agopian said.

But there's always the problem of what to do if there is no custody order. "The abduction of a child by a parent may fall outside the law," he said. "Many cases screened for prosecution fail to meet specific criteria defined by law. The abduction may have been committed prior to a custody order. If a custody order *has* been issued, the offending parent may not have been informed of such a judgment prior to the snatching. Or, third, the offending parent may also have been acting in accordance with a second, conflicting custody order obtained from another jurisdiction."

And there is still the problem of finding the abductor. "Nearly a quarter of the cases studied did not move beyond the issuance of a bench warrant for the offender's arrest," Agopian said. "If an offending parent leaves the jurisdiction and is not involved in future criminality and felony charges have not been filed, he or she is well insulated from prosecution. Should an offending parent choose not to seek legal custody in another jurisdiction, the chance of locating that parent becomes remote.

"Satisfied with stealing the child, the offending parent's failure to seek legal custody reduces contact with the criminal justice system. Increased mobility and the ease of adopting new identities and integrating into new communities further enhance the offender's escape from criminal action," he said.

Often parents want their children back and don't wish to press charges. It is the threat of jail or a fine that parents hope will force the abducting parent to return the child. In other cases, parents may want to get together and reconcile. They feel criminal warrants could make their spouse angry and force him or her to run further away.

"The parties may be separated or attempting to reconcile the marriage and the filing of criminal charges may rupture the already delicate relationship between the parties," Agopian said. "The strict application of the criminal process by a prosecutor is, therefore, rare."

Parents of stolen children are luckier in California than in many other states. Each county district attorney's office has a section to handle child stealing. Parents first file complaints with local police, then bring copies of those complaints to the custody investigator in the district attorney's office. This investigator then will go with parents before a judge and ask for felony warrants.

These warrants, like felony charges for other crimes, go on a national police computer, which all states use to keep track of persons wanted for felonies. Police in other states who stop someone for traffic violations can check with this computer to see if that person is wanted for child stealing.

California police will notify the victimized parent that his or her former spouse has been arrested. Police in other states may do this, but often don't. They've arrested abductors and let them go after posting bail, before victimized parents can fly in to recover their stolen children.

In California, as in other states, though, there is still the problem of prosecuting abductors. Judges there seem as lenient as judges in the rest of the country, and frequently won't punish child stealers. They'll allow abductors to have overnight, unsupervised visitation, even if they've been found guilty of child stealing.

California's laws, again, work only for parents who have custody. They won't work if there are no custody papers. They are also intended to work for parents who have visitation orders. But sometimes law enforcement authorities feel they have their hands full with enforcing custody and don't have time to enforce visitation. Nevertheless, California has the most progressive child stealing laws in the country, and should serve as a model for other states to follow.

10

International Child Stealing

Parents whose children have been taken out of the country have it even harder, legally, than parents whose stolen children stay in America. They must find their former husbands or wives themselves and take them to court in the new country. But it will be up to a court in the foreign land to decide whether to honor a custody order granted in the United States, if there is one.

If there isn't a custody order from America, there could be a whole new hearing about whom a child or children should live with. But even if there is such an order, giving custody to the victimized parent, the judge on foreign soil might reverse it, especially if the absconding parent is a native of the second country.

One New York City mother lost her two children when her ex-husband took them to Athens. Even though she had custody in New York State, she lost it in Greece. Parents with children stolen to Italy and Germany had similar experiences. All had to appear in courts in Europe. All lost. All had former spouses who were citizens of those foreign countries.

Mothers and fathers agree that stealing back their children is the best method of recovery in these cases. However, this can be hard if the absconding parent holds passports for the children. A victimized parent could travel great distances, even see the children where they live (but often not be allowed to take them out of the house or apartment where they now reside), yet not be able to steal them back without passports. They wouldn't be allowed to leave the country unless they hired professional smugglers and had duplicate passports.

People have tried to get the U.S. government to recover their children, especially if absconding parents have felony warrants against them. But it's hard, almost impossible. Our government has to ask the foreign government to send home the children, to extradite the absconding parent because he or she is charged with a felony in America.

The United States would have to pay for sending home those absconding parents, which would be expensive. Our country also doesn't send home child stealers from other countries, because stealing children isn't a felony here.

"Take, for example, a case in which the Canadian government sought extradition of a Canadian citizen living in San Francisco for violations of a kidnapping law," said Senator Malcolm Wallop, sponsor of the Senate bill to stop child stealing. "Even though the Canada-U.S. treaty specifically lists child snatching as an extraditable offense, the United States refused to extradite on the grounds that there was no comparable felony offense in the United States," Wallop said.

Parents have tried to have our State Department extradite abductors in order to avoid a new trial on foreign soil. One woman who tried, and finally succeeded, was a California mother whose children were stolen to Argentina.

"Although there existed treaties [regarding extradition of criminals] between Argentina and the United States, the State Department referred me to a Los Angeles district attorney extradition specialist who kept insisting that there were none, and who, consistently, for two years, refused me any help," she said.

Finally she took him a translated copy of those treaties, plus letters from her attorney and from a judge in Argentina, who was waiting for a signal from the United States before he would decide whether or not to uphold her custody order.

"The advice from the State Department and the district attorney was, 'If you want to see your children again, you will have to find them and kidnap them back,' " she said.

This mother spent two and a half years in Argentine courts, went there ten times and spent over $250,000, she said, employing over eighteen lawyers. She was able, finally, to get the extradition process started and the Argentine judge let her have her children.

"I had to hire a private plane and pilot to fly us out before my ex-husband filed an appeal from the extradition," she said. "We left the same day the Argentine judge signed the papers.

"The important point is that the request for extradition is what was helpful in getting my children back," she said.

Another Californian was not as lucky.

She sent her three small children back to New York for a summer visit and her ex-husband didn't return them. She got a child-stealing warrant on him and learned he'd gotten passports for their children by claiming the original ones, which she had, were stolen.

"I had passports in my possession and was naive enough to believe the State Department wouldn't issue illegal passports. I was told my ex-husband had obtained just such passports. The State Department wrote me that, even so, his second passports were good for ninety days, and they would renew them for one year," she said.

"I asked how they could issue double passports and they told me anyone could. They are unable to check," she said.

"By then we had already spent one hundred fifty thousand dollars obeying the law. My ex-husband didn't then, doesn't now, and probably never will," she said.

A national magazine interviewed her and printed pictures of her children. Someone wrote her from South America that her children were in Brazil. She asked California and the federal government to send her children home. Several senators and congressmen wrote to the Secretary of State, asking for help.

They were turned down.

"The governor of California had already signed extradition papers allowing California to send a police officer, an assistant district attorney and two special agents to Brazil to arrest my ex-husband and return my children," she said. "The Brazilian consul general in Los Angeles had already indicated his government would honor the request.

"The Secretary of State then announced he believed there was good reason *not* to honor any treaty that mentions child stealing," she said.

This mother finally recovered her children years later because of the felony child-stealing warrant she had obtained. When her husband and the children came back to America from Canada, U.S. officials stopped them at the border, held the father because of the warrant, and the mother flew there with her custody papers.

She explained it was that felony warrant, not any civil papers, such as habeas corpus, requests for new hearings, orders to enforce custody, which brought home her children.

Yet many parents don't have custody when former spouses steal children and can't get such felony warrants. Or, if they live in one of the states where snatching is only a misdemeanor, they can only get that kind of a warrant, which police can't send to border patrols or to foreign authorities.

There is still the problem of finding stolen children, though. Searching the entire globe can be impossible, unless someone is wealthy and has time to travel extensively.

11

Parents on Their Own

Some parents are lucky. They are able to bring their children home with little expense. They don't hire lawyers or investigators; they become their own detectives. They realize no one *else* will recover their children. They must do it themselves, by jungle rules. As child stealers think of ways to hide, parents learn how to find them. They trace abductors through jobs, schools, old friends, new spouses, thinking quickly, and acting alone. Sometimes they must become amateur actors and actresses to find their children.

A mother in Syracuse, New York, found her former husband and their two children in San Jose, California, through his union. Tom Devereau, thirty-four, a sheetmetal worker, left home with the children before there were any legal papers. His wife, Jean, thirty, worked as a bank teller. She knew her husband wouldn't transfer money from their account because she could learn where it went.

But Tom needed money. There were no relatives to support him. She called his union office and pretended she worked for a different bank and was checking on Tom Devereau because he'd applied for a loan. Could the union verify his employment?

A secretary there said he'd left his job with an automaker in Syracuse, but that his union membership records had been sent to a local branch of the same union in California. She gave Jean Devereau the name and address of that local.

Jean then phoned the California union office, and pretended she worked for a bank in San Francisco. She told a similar story: Tom Devereau recently had moved to the Bay Area and could they verify where he worked and lived?

"I didn't want them to think I was fishing," Jean Devereau said. "So I acted like I knew what I was doing. I gave them a phony address in Palo Alto and a phony employer. The woman at the local was helpful and corrected me, saying he worked for a manufacturing plant in San Jose and lived in the same city."

Three days later Jean and her brother flew to San Francisco, rented a car, and drove south to San Jose. "We thought he must put our children in day care while he worked," Jean said. "My brother learned that his address was for an apartment. Tom wasn't living with friends or a family who could watch the kids when he worked."

Her brother watched Tom's apartment early one morning, followed him to a day care center, saw him leave the children there at seven thirty.

Jean recovered them without a fight. She showed the director birth certificates of her children and had her brother call Tom at work, just before their plane left San Francisco.

"My only expenses were plane tickets and motels for a couple of days," Jean said.

Other parents have found their children through new wives or husbands of their former spouses. A Long Island mother knew her ex-husband had remarried and that his new wife had an eight-year-old son in a local elementary school. She called the school several days after her ex-husband stole her two children, who were six and seven years old. The school told her that records for her ex-husband's stepson had been sent to a school in Tampa, Florida.

She figured her children would be in the same school. She was right.

"My ex-husband hadn't asked for school records of *our*

children to be transferred anywhere," the mother, Josette Levine, twenty-nine, said. "But when I learned where his stepson was in school, I felt my children would be there, too. It was my only lead and I had to check it out."

With an uncle, she flew to Tampa. He called the Florida school and said he was an assistant school principal on Long Island who wanted to know if the stepson's records had arrived. A secretary told him they had. Then he asked if records of two *other* children had arrived and gave their names and their former school on Long Island.

The secretary said the records hadn't arrived, but the children had. Josette, who had custody of her children, went to the school and asked to see them. The principal allowed her to and she brought her children home.

"It took playacting," she said. "My ex-husband was a car salesman and [the people at] his old job said they didn't know where he went. So I tried the school and was lucky. I'm glad he'd remarried and had that stepson."

Parents sometimes steal children without thinking. They make no plans, act impulsively, hide with their closest friends. These abductors can be easy to find, but recovering stolen children from them might take deceit.

One mother, Debra Rockne, twenty-seven, was a part-time hairdresser who lived in Los Angeles with her husband, Anthony, thirty-one, an auto mechanic, and their eighteen-month-old son, Tony. Their marriage faltered. Anthony couldn't keep a job. They moved to Long Island in October 1979, and lived with Debra's parents. But it didn't work; they still fought, and living with her parents seemed to make it worse.

On a Saturday night in November 1979, they decided to move. Anthony had a pickup truck. The couple took their baby and found a motel. Debra got out, walked into the office, told the clerk she and her husband wanted a suite for two weeks.

Anthony drove off while she was inside.

Debra didn't even see his taillights, couldn't know which way he'd gone. She screamed. Their baby was so little. Most of his clothes were at her mother's house. She called her father, who took her home.

There were no divorce papers, no custody order. "The hardest part, after realizing I might not see my baby again," she said, "was waiting. We figured Anthony would need several days to settle down. The only places I could think of where he might go would be to his mother's in Oakland, California, or to friends we knew in Los Angeles."

She didn't call California right away, though. His mother might tell him Debra was on his trail, and she had to think if their friends would side with Anthony or her.

"After five days I called my best friend in Los Angeles," Debra said. "We ruled out his mother because she was elderly. I had my friend get her boyfriend, who had a motorcycle, to drive by the homes of other people we knew. He did and saw Anthony's truck in one of their driveways, which made Anthony angry because he thought the motorcyclist had been sent to spy on him.

"He called and said I shouldn't spy on him," Debra said. "But I felt he still loved me. So I played dumb, asked him back, said I couldn't live without him."

Anthony fell for it and told her to fly out. They would try to reconcile.

"I knew we couldn't, but he had the baby," Debra said. "I went out there and stayed with my best friend. Anthony and Tony were with other friends, who took his side. We agreed I could come over and visit."

He let her see their baby for one hour the first day, but wouldn't let her take him out of the house. Debra went over the next day and stayed four hours. She did this for a week, until Anthony relaxed and said he didn't think she was going to leave him. They made plans to live together again in Los Angeles.

"I felt we couldn't do it, though," Debra said, "not after

what he'd done to me. I'd be stuck in L.A. where I was—visiting my own baby, but never being allowed to take him out or bring him home. I convinced everyone I was broke and couldn't afford plane fare back to Kennedy Airport."

Finally, after ten days, Debra saw her chance. "Anthony went back to one of his old jobs and his friends agreed I could take Tony out in the stroller. I called a cab as soon as I was around the corner and got on the next plane leaving Los Angeles. It was to Sacramento, California, but I didn't care. Now that I'm home on Long Island, I feel bad about telling Anthony I wanted to patch up our marriage. But my baby meant more to me."

Searching alone takes courage and humility, an ability to act gently and not let bitterness get in the way of finding and recovering the children. But most of all it takes strength to go it alone when no agency, public or private, will help.

Another woman who did it on her own was Linda Nowell, twenty-eight, a housewife and part-time waitress in a diner in Mastic Beach, New York. Her ex-husband, Sam, thirty-two, worked in the air-conditioning and heating business in Brooklyn. They have two sons, Charlie, five, and Eddie, two. Linda and Sam Nowell separated in the summer of 1979. On Labor Day of that year, Sam came out to Mastic Beach from Brooklyn to take Charlie for a few days.

He didn't return him.

Linda had a court order giving her temporary custody and child support for both boys and hoped the courts would find her husband to collect her money.

"It wasn't what I *really* wanted," she said. "I wanted my son, but there was no other way I could find anyone to help. There was a possible address for Sam in Colorado. I told family court he had left with my son and I wanted it brought into the Colorado courts.

"Their attitude was that if he wasn't at that address, they weren't going to look for him," she said.

Court clerks in Yaphank, New York, told her what judges,

police, lawyers, and other victimized parents had said: Get your son yourself.

"They also told me that I should go there myself," Linda Nowell said. "Yaphank told me that if I went out there and kidnapped him back, I would not be breaking the law. One person in family court told me that possession is nine-tenths of the law. Since my husband had the child, he, in effect, had custody."

She didn't have money. Five lawyers wanted three hundred dollars to draw up divorce papers, since she wasn't legally divorced yet, only separated.

They told her she could only ask for custody of Eddie.

"I couldn't sue for custody of Charlie here, they told me," she said. "I told them that Sam had kidnapped him and they told me a parent cannot kidnap his own child."

Her husband knew she didn't have money to find him. "It would have meant flying to Denver," Linda Nowell said. "Then taking another flight to a local airport. That would have cost three hundred fifty dollars, plus tax, just for the fare. Then I would have had to rent a car, pay for motels and eating, so you're talking about at least five hundred. Only for one week, too."

Linda Nowell figured Sam might be in Colorado because he'd gone there when they'd separated before and had sent a letter to Charlie. "It had a return address from Montrose, Colorado," she said. "I don't know why, but I just happened to keep that envelope. It was from a trailer camp and was the address I gave family court. But they never followed it up."

Upset at losing her child, Linda Nowell took a second part-time job in a delicatessen, off the books, and kept control of herself.

"I called the trailer park and got the manager and she said he wasn't there anymore, but that she could ask around. I told her not to do that, because I didn't want Sam to know I was on his trail," she said.

So she waited. It was hard.

"Those ten months were heartbreaking," Linda Nowell said. "I couldn't sleep or eat and I got along with nobody. I was defensive, and had guilt for letting it happen. Other people reacted the same way. Like, how could I have been so stupid and let him see Charlie? My friends are secure. They have their families and husbands and can't see anything like this happening. They attacked me, saying I had brought it on myself."

Then in April 1980, she got a break. Her husband called: Charlie wanted to speak with his mother. "Sam knew I couldn't leave Long Island," she said. "I had my other son and the house. He figured I wouldn't go out there and felt safe."

They called from a pay phone. Linda was humble. She just wanted to tell her son that she loved him and hoped he was all right and didn't argue with Sam. Charlie came on.

"I kept him talking past the three minutes," she said. "The operator cut in and said, 'You're on overtime.' When my husband came back on, he asked if she had cut in and I told him no. When he hung up, there was money due. The operator came on again and I said she could bill the overtime to me. My heart was pounding and I tried not to cry or stammer. I asked where the call was from and she said Montrose, Colorado.

He was still there, although not at that trailer park. Should she call other trailer parks? How many were there?

Sam's brother wouldn't tell Linda where her child was. He did tell her Sam worked as a carpet installer, though.

"I got out a map, then," Linda Nowell said. "From the telephone directory in my local library I looked up names of carpet companies near Montrose. I called several of them and found out where he worked. I wrote him a letter and he called again. This time I talked about how we should try to work things out, that Charlie should be with his brother and in his own home, that if Sam brought him back he could see him any time he wanted."

She lived on hope now. She'd made contact. There was a thaw. She didn't want to scare her husband. But it hurt deeply.

"It was the hope of getting him back which kept me going," she said. "Also, people who were close to me felt sooner or later Charlie would want to see his mother. Talking on the phone with him helped, but, in another way, it was devastating, because at first he didn't want to come home.

"And he started calling me by my first name. He'd say 'Linda,' instead of 'Mom.' He referred to the girl who took care of him as his mother. This hurt. Each time I spoke with him I had to swallow that. I didn't want to scold him and tried to keep him talking."

Which she did. There were five calls in April and May 1980. Linda Nowell tried to keep calm. The abduction had hurt her family, too. There was sorrow, anger, guilt, all of which she kept out of her voice. There was just love.

"I kept telling Charlie we missed him," she said, "and hoped he was fine. But my family was depressed, also. My mother had just gotten over a heart attack and I kept it from her and my father as long as I could when Charlie was first taken.

"When I did tell them, I said Sam had taken him on a trip for a couple of months. But my parents asked why Charlie wasn't home for Christmas. It was heartbreaking when I told them he was gone. My mother asked, 'What do you mean *gone*? He's your son.'

"I worried all the time about whether I would ever see him again, but I couldn't tell my mother that. She got on my nerves, always asking, 'What do you mean *gone*?' I fought with her and told her first to shut up and then that it was none of her business and finally that I needed her, and she understood.

"What if I didn't see him until he was sixteen? I might never know him. I also worried because Charlie used to get sick and run fevers," she said.

There was a break in early June 1980. Charlie wanted to come home. Sam's brother went to Colorado. "Charlie was giving my husband's girlfriend problems," Linda Nowell said. "Also, Sam got adverse comments from his family. They felt he was wrong in what he did."

Sam's brother brought Charlie home. Mother and son saw each other for the first time in ten months.

"The first thing we did was open his Christmas presents," she said. "We had a party."

12

Custody Vigilantes

Many parents hire professionals to steal or to recover their children. Some are licensed private investigators. Others make their living recovering kids, either through courts or by physically taking them. They work out of motels and travel alone; none have licenses, as do normal private eyes who advertise publicly; some carry weapons. They claim to work only for parents who have custody, distraught mothers or fathers whose children have been spirited off by an angry ex-spouse. But there is evidence that some actually do the initial snatch as well.

Some have false identification papers, wear disguises, carry burglar's tools. They work by themselves and are hard to find. Parents hear their names by word of mouth, or through divorce reform groups, usually fathers' rights organizations. They call themselves "custody vigilantes" and cherish their image of idealistic mercenaries, paid kidnappers for a noble cause.

John Raleigh is one. He has a ten-year-old son and a nine-year-old daughter, and worked for a wholesale grocery store in Belmont, New York. He became a custody vigilante as the result of his own experience. After Raleigh's wife disappeared with their children, he spent five years trying to find them. He quit his job and has had custody of his children since shortly after they were taken. During the time he roamed the country trying to find his own children, he also began helping other parents find theirs.

Losing his children made him want to help other parents in similar straits. He said he's been involved with about six hundred child stealings and has actually picked up children about thirty-five or forty times. He got into the "child recovery business," he said, because the system couldn't work. He realized he'd have to find his children himself and decided to help others at the same time.

"I spent a lot of money through the legal process, thinking there was some recourse that I could take that would locate my children and enforce the custody decree. I spent thousands of dollars before I realized that wasn't possible. Then I hired several private detectives, who took my money and gave me nothing. I got the feeling, as most parents do, that I was the only one who was facing this frustrating hell on earth.

"Since that time I've been doing what I can to help other victimized parents through the legal process, if that's possible, and if that's not possible, I have helped some recover their children through other means."

Those "other means" involve grabbing kids off streets, out of playgrounds, wherever. He said he wouldn't try a recovery if it might hurt a child. And he thought parents had to be sure about his recovery plans before picking up children.

"I'd rather spend an extra few days and wait for a safe opportunity," he said, "than be hasty and get into something risky. It takes patience, and there are those who don't agree with that part of it. But if I knew where my children were and wasn't able to get them back legally, I would be faced with the same decision. Should I let them stay there if the law isn't going to help, or should I try and get them back through some other means?"

Raleigh advises trying the legal process first. "We have referral attorneys in several parts of the country," he said, "attorneys who we can go to and feel our way and see what the attitude in the local courts is. If we have a pretty good shot at getting a child back legally, then we'll go legally. But if the attorney says we don't, we just get the child any way we can."

He told of a case in Tennessee. "A mother had custody in Michigan," he said, "and the father stole their two little girls and fled to Memphis. The mother went down to enforce her custody order and police refused to help her." After a frustrating and futile experience with the courts, Tammy North hired Raleigh to recover her kids.

They first went to a local court with her custody papers. A judge said she'd voluntarily let her children visit their father so there was no abduction.

Raleigh checked Tammy's divorce papers to make sure they were valid and spoke with a second attorney in Tennessee. But nothing could be done. Tammy and her mother went to Memphis with him and they watched her ex-husband's house for three days. They learned the best time to snatch the girls was when they were dropped off by a bus after Bible school.

Raleigh said the house next to where her ex-husband lived was vacant and for sale. He tried to rent it, but couldn't. He and Tammy North asked to inspect it, though, and waited until the school bus came by in the afternoon.

"Timing must be exact," he said, "even to the right second. We watched the street and wanted to grab the kids without causing a disturbance in the neighborhood.

"The bus driver didn't know what to think," Raleigh said. "We always assume people nearby will think it's a real kidnapping, and I feel that driver thought it was."

But they got to their car and drove to a second one parked a few minutes away. In several hours they were in Arkansas. Raleigh called Memphis police to say the children were with their mother. He mailed copies of the custody papers to both police and FBI.

Tammy had taken off her wig during the ride in the first car. Her daughters were happy to see her. Their father had told them Tammy didn't want to see them anymore.

"They said they were scared when we first got them," Raleigh said, "but they calmed down after a few minutes."

He said police arrived soon after, and had a helicopter trying to spot their getaway car.

Raleigh is happy to help parents, even though he dislikes the vigilante approach. "I detest the fact that any parent is forced to go out and snatch his or her own children off the street in order to enforce a custody decree. It shouldn't be done that way."

He also points out that anyone can grab children. "It doesn't take some private investigator or myself to do it," he said. "A great many parents can do it themselves." Raleigh differs from others in his field because he supports the passage of laws to stop the problem of child stealing.

Asking for money was hard for him. "The people I've helped, I don't have the heart to ask them for money," he said. "You must remember, these people don't have any money. They've spent it all on lawyers and private investigators. You do people a service when you tell them not to use private investigators. I've seen so many of them just get taken over the coals by these private eyes. They're vultures."

John Raleigh, a man who has spent many years recovering children for other parents, found his own children by himself. In 1973, his wife disappeared with their children, a boy and a girl. He ultimately found them through phone bills. He would check long distance calls made by his wife's relatives, doing this for the entire five years he was on the road. He could get three months' phone bills for $180, he said, by bribing a phone company employee.

"It wasn't one thing that led to her," he said. "It was an accumulation of work, chasing down leads. I documented everything. It was like a puzzle. A few times I was on her trail and knew where she was, but I didn't have her alias. I even had the city sometimes. She was in Providence, Rhode Island, for a year and a half once, but I couldn't turn her up.

When she first vanished, she lived in a commune in Massachusetts.

"Then at Christmastime 1977, I got some information through a trash watch," he said. This is going through garbage cans of friends and relatives who might know where someone is and looking for something with a return address. It is best, he said, to check phone bills and sift through trash around holidays, when people contact relatives. He said to do it at night when people sleep.

"I suspected for some time she was in Billings, Montana, because I knew her boyfriend's family lived there," he said. "It was in Missouri—St. Louis, to be exact—that I got the information I wanted. I'd been doing trash watches for years. I found a little cardboard box that a woman's writing paper would be sent in. On the outside of the box, in my wife's handwriting, it said, 'For Mom.' It was purchased from a company in Billings.

"In June [1978] I turned up an alias. She actually had two. Then I really zeroed in on the address, checking telephone books, phone company and power company records, confirmed the address, and went out there. She had changed her name and the children's names and had enrolled them in school under fictitious names.

"I explored my situation with two attorneys in Montana and they both told me that with my temporary custody order, plus the fact that my children were gone five years, time was against me. Montana wouldn't enforce my New York decree, they said. Both attorneys told me the same thing: 'If you want to litigate further, my advice is to take physical custody of the children and return them to New York State.' That's exactly what I did."

Raleigh told what happened when he saw his children for the first time in five years. "My brother and I did it. It wasn't difficult. There was no confrontation. I was out there [in the area where they lived] before school started in the morning.

My wife and her boyfriend were working and the children were in the care of a baby-sitter, which they were most of the time.

"The kids were about two blocks from the sitter's house, in a schoolyard. They were with another little girl, and my brother and I recognized them as we pulled into the parking lot alongside the school. We walked up to them and started talking and I had all kinds of pictures which were taken before they disappeared. I had books they used to read, too, and pictures they had drawn, loads of stuff that would help refresh their memories. We sat there talking for about five or six minutes, telling them who we were. My son remembered us, so there was no problem, and we coaxed them into the car and were on our way."

There are some vigilantes who try to use child stealing to focus public attention on the problem and thus help change laws. One of the most active of these is Eugene "Mean Gene" Austin, who has lived on the road for most of his fifty-six years. He has recovered children longer than anyone else, and he likes what he does.

Austin is the first one to tell you that, too.

He created the name "Mean Gene" himself, and tries to live up to it by wearing green work clothes, which make him look like a janitor, or "an old wino," as he says. He has opinions about everything and loves to argue. No one can tell him what to do.

For three hundred dollars, plus expenses, Gene Austin will go anywhere, anytime, to help find snatched children. He's been on "Sixty Minutes," "The Tomorrow Show," "The Mac-Neil/Lehrer Report," and many local television shows. He has a stack of newspaper clippings, his "ego file," two inches thick, and doesn't mind if he's hard to get along with (*The Wall Street Journal* once called him "abrasive"). His wife is a semi-invalid; he has three grown children whom he doesn't allow reporters or writers to mention; he calls home at six o'clock every Thursday evening to see what mail there is for him.

Actually, he doesn't call his house in Foley, Missouri, but a neighbor's house, where his wife waits with letters from all over the country. He claims he doesn't have a home phone because, if he did, it would be bugged.

Also, the reason he can't go home, he says, is because of an assassin in a white car parked in front of his house. The mob is out to get him, he claims, because he once recovered a child for a father whose ex-wife was a prostitute with the mob. Austin is hazy about the father's name, however, because, he insists, if he told someone, that someone might be slain. As for his tapped phone, when he had it, either the CIA, FBI, or Defense Intelligence Agency listened in on him, he claims, once.

Austin is the best-known child snatcher in the country. His income is modest. There are detective agencies that flourish in the business of child recoveries, but not Austin. He is a crusader, he says, willing to turn the country upside down for a cause, any cause. Money is not important. Ending child stealing is.

"If I wanted to do this for pay, I could get rich," he said.

"I believe in what the man says he's doing because many of our custody laws are atrocious," said one Miami prosecutor. "His methods, however, can be unconstitutional and violent."

Austin started child snatching in Omaha, Nebraska, in 1964. "In those early days," he said, "I had a married couple come to me. The wife's grandparents had broken into the house, beat up the baby-sitter, grabbed the child, and took off to another county. They had a court order from the state supreme court to return the child, which the sheriff flatly refused to enforce.

"So I said, 'Hell, if it's legal for them to steal the child, it's legal for us to steal him back.' I got five men, went down and locked Grandma in her own basement and took the kid back to his own home. Another man and I sat in the boy's house with a shotgun for two days, while the grandmother, who'd been released from her cellar, and her friends prowled the grounds with *their* shotguns. They were out on the lawn, religious fanatics."

His reputation grew from then on. "It seemed like I kept getting them [child-snatching cases]. I spent from 1964 until 1970 collecting cases, just like that, and divorce cases, too. I went to legislators. I went to Congress. I went to judges. I went to the media. I went every place I could think of and a hell of a lot of exotic ones, too.

"Nobody would do a damn thing. They wouldn't even write articles. So in 1970 I said, 'All right, you sons of bitches, now I'm gonna teach you a lesson. We're going to revert to the old mule training method.' That training," he explains, "is to hit them between the eyes with a bunch of snatches and then tell them what I want. I started snatching back children and every time I'd walk into the local newspaper office."

One of his important cases was helping a father from St. Louis recover his three-year-old son from Miami, Florida. The father, George Hall, was a twenty-two-year-old bricklayer; his former wife, Betty, twenty-three, took their son in August 1976. Austin claimed Florida police wouldn't recognize a Missouri custody order which gave the boy to his father.

"I went into Miami and pulled that big hairy stunt [recovering a child] with Betty Hall," he said. "That was a big one, that hit *The Wall Street Journal*, that hit everything. The father was given legal custody in St. Louis. The mother snatched the kid and we knew she was in Miami, but we didn't know where.

"The district attorney in St. Louis issued a warrant and a police officer from St. Louis County hand-carried it to Miami. But police there just laughed him out of town. We found her because we knew the name of her boyfriend and we found *him*. Well, Miami wouldn't even go out and serve her. So George came back and got me.

"It was a beautiful case," Austin said. "We staked out where she lived for six days and rented an apartment right across from her back fence. She knew we were in town and she had the child stashed. We put George's brother in one car and George and I took the rented car and watched. Inside half an hour one day, here she comes with the kid. We saw her get out of the car with the kid and we drove up and George got out and wrestled her to the ground, with the kid between them, and she was fighting tooth and toenail and screaming, and here comes her boyfriend out of the house with a baseball bat.

"I fired a shot across his nose [a punch], but that didn't work. So he came at me and I spotted a tree and faked him out so he would hit the tree and, by God, he did. This was right on the front lawn, with the whole neighborhood watching.

"Then I walked over and gave her this real little shot of paralyzer. It wasn't half what the court claimed, just enough to make her let loose. George grabbed the kid and jumped in the car and we got our asses out of there. We took the rental car and zig-zagged across the country and went to Atlanta, Georgia."

Austin likes publicity and the Miami case gave him a good chance. "We went into Atlanta and I walked into the newspaper office and told them we had just kidnapped a kid right off the street in Miami," he said.

"Poor George, he liked to drop his jawbone. He wanted to go home and I said, 'Hell, no, we're going to use this one. This is the one that is going to bust them.'" Austin figures the more sensational the publicity, the more people will recognize the seriousness of the problem and the absurdity of the laws.

"The police in Atlanta came in," Austin said, "and we called their district attorney and, man, did we get a story.

Then I went home and wrote a letter to the Miami *Herald* and bragged about what I had done. I called the courts corrupt and lambasted everybody. I wanted to be arrested and it took four months for them to arrest me.

"The charges were aggravated assault, aggravated battery, and child torture. I had affirmative defenses for everything except a minor misdemeanor. They didn't charge her [Betty Hall] with violating that custody order from Missouri."

Austin was extradited from Missouri on a child torture charge, convicted on one count of aggravated assault, and sentenced to thirty months in jail and thirty months on probation. He appealed, and a divorced men's group came up with $7,500 for his bail.

He said his conviction was overturned on appeal, the charge reduced to simple assault, and the final actual sentence was time served. That was about four and a half months in jail, which he'd already spent waiting for the trial.

George Hall was glad to have his son home despite Austin's flamboyance. The recovery scared him, but he was happy. "Austin drove me crazy and scared me to death," Hall said. "But I'd already tried everything—police, courts, lawyers, private detectives, and they just took more money and more money—five thousand dollars in all. Gene gave me back my boy and took one hundred dollars."

Austin spoke of his family law council and said it has people all over the country who help him. "I stay with people I work with," he said, "and in safe houses on the road. I have about twenty-four hundred houses that I know of. I've got a network all over the country and I keep adding a few more names every time I turn around. I'm trying to work out a complete network that I can cross the country with. Those damn motels are murder.

"I try to cut expenses. I stay a night or two here and there and slowly, but surely, I'm building them up. All of the people I stay with have been victims at one time or another. I'm teaching some of them how to do their own searches."

Newspaper and magazine articles about his recoveries have appeared in periodicals in Los Angeles, Denver, San Jose, California, Philadelphia, Pennsylvania, and Kansas City. They appear frequently. He is good copy. Stories on him brighten a newspaper. Headlines call him "The Meanest Man in Town" and "A Pro at Child Snatching." One reporter in Miami won an award for feature writing because of an article about him.

Many articles run his picture: his face craggy, wearing glasses, his hair crew cut. All quote from parents he's helped. Some include statements from district attorneys, sheriffs, and police about what Austin has done. Others say how he dislikes bills in Congress to make snatching a federal crime.

He doesn't support the bill introduced by Senator Wallop because, Austin claims, the United States Supreme Court has ruled that domestic relations should be left to individual states. Austin also opposes a similar bill in the House of Representatives sponsored by Congressman Charles Bennett of Florida.

He hasn't made a vigilante recovery recently, he said, because now judges frown on "back-snatching." "They fear it could hurt children and might punish a parent for doing it, even though he or she had custody originally," he said. Austin, perhaps mellowing, said people should only go through the courts now and never grab children off streets.

What is his answer then, if he frowns on recoveries?

Austin wants to take a test case to the Supreme Court, which, he said, might change the Court's position on allowing states to rule by themselves on child custody affairs. It would say that the federal government has the right to enforce state custody orders and could actually decide which state's order should be upheld if there was a conflict. However, he was vague about what case he would use to try and convince the Court there was already a precedent for the federal government to solve domestic disputes between individual states.

One summer, he went to Long Island to help a Nassau County mother recover her two-year-old daughter from the state of Washington. Austin lived with Penny Watson and her children from a former marriage for about eight months, through fall and winter, helping her attorney with legal research. It was an experience.

"He had to dominate every single aspect of living," she said, laughing. "*Everything*, the greatest dictator ever known. He told us how to clean the pans, how to wash out the sink, how to clean the drainboard. He knew everything about refrigerators and stoves."

In many ways it was a joyful experience for her, she said, because he never gave up. Also, he was handy around her home. "He redid the whole sewer system in my house," Penny said. She had him living in the basement on a pull-out bed, warming himself with a small electric heater, which cost her an extra sixty dollars a month in electric bills. They kept out of each other's way part of the time because Austin went to bed very late, she said, and slept late each morning.

But he was like a growing, hyperactive child to feed.

"He has seven eggs for breakfast," Penny said. "He ate two meals a day and could eat like I don't know what. He *loved* to eat. Sugar was his favorite. He had five pounds of it a week, said he needed it to live on, putting it on everything. He loved gloppy desserts, three scoops of ice cream, and pancakes with everything, too, floating in syrup.

"He was a walking dictionary and encyclopedia," she said, a man who was never quiet. He could talk about the Russian Revolution or about how to rewire every electrical outlet in her home. He was never still, always jingled change in his pockets, walked around, searched for a soapbox to stand on, an audience to preach at, some fixture to replace, she said.

Penny Watson got through the year her child was

snatched with prayer, she said, and is a born-again Christian. "I feel I've met God now and I know things about life I never knew before. I'm a very happy person," she said.

Her advice was to love, not hate, people, and, she said, being around Austin taught her to be tolerant. She had warm feelings for him, the man with two suitcases and a cardboard filing cabinet for a traveling office.

"I admire him more than anything else. He got my child back," she said. "What other man in the history of the world would go find my child, but Gene Austin? And because of that I love him more than anyone. Nothing can replace him."

13

Private Investigators

Not every parent recovers children with the help of friends or relatives, or has a John Raleigh or Gene Austin to travel the country for them. Many hire licensed private investigators who claim they will find and bring home abducted children. Few investigators can, however. The usual experience, as with lawyers, is that parents spend money and have nothing to show for it, because most investigators usually prefer to handle insurance claims and divorces. Child recovery is a rare and difficult, but growing, specialty.

One investigator who helps recover children for parents in New York is George Cerone of Great Neck. Cerone claims to have made about seventy recoveries, mostly up and down the East Coast, but some as far away as California and Texas.

Cerone makes a living snatching children. Unlike vigilantes, though, he has a license from the New York Department of State. He will try to find someone—the most difficult part of child stealing—for $1,500 and charges another $1,500 to recover a child, plus expenses.

"It comes out to around five to six thousand dollars all told," he said. "These figures can rise, of course, if more detective work is involved and there are more expenses on the road."

Cerone explained how he sets up a recovery: He spends about three days planning it, and takes two people from his agency, besides the victimized parent. He has to be cautious.

"When you're operating in another state," he said, "there are no laws to protect you. Basically, you're a kidnapper, and you have to pull these things off to cause a minimum of confusion and attention. After I've found the child, I make two different travel plans. The first is to get into the state [where the absconding parent is] and the second, of course, is to get out. I generally base my return on open reservations.

"When we get to where we are going, we take a motel room, preferably within a mile or two of where we want to make the recovery," he said. Cerone studies major access routes in the city or area, checks secondary roads, all methods of escape. He calls local police and asks what the traffic conditions are at different times of the day.

"The reason I do this is so we won't get caught short trying to get away, with the possibility of somebody following us, or winding up on a one-way street, going the wrong way," he said. Setting up the getaway takes no more than an hour. He makes a map of the area and drives the streets or highways, sees which exits lead to the airport, which ones go to his motel, marks these exits on his map.

"I then take a second motel, often within a mile or so of the original motel," he said. "I make a reservation under a phony name and pay for it. That's in the event for some reason the first motel gets involved. Somebody gets a plate number or police happen to see our car. I always have a second place to go, to hide with the child."

He uses two cars. The actual snatch is done in one car. A mile or so away is the second car, hidden. He will grab a child, go to the second car, get in with his client and the child, and have the first car driven off in another direction. One of his men drives that first car twenty or thirty miles, stops, calls the office in Great Neck, and they tell him how long to wait until returning it and flying home.

"As soon as a recovery is made, I notify home base," Cerone said, "and tell them about how long I'll need to leave the state. They tell our first driver to wait until everything is clear before he can leave. This is done to confuse law enforcement people, if they become involved. All they'll be able to trace or find is that first car."

If he plans on ultimately leaving the state by plane, he makes several separate airline reservations in advance. "Let's say I'm going to St. Louis from here, New York," he said. "If I think the job will be done on Thursday, I'll make reservations to come home in my client's name on two or three airlines. Let's say from St. Louis to Miami, New York and San Francisco. This way if the other parent starts checking airlines after the recovery, he or she will find reservations to every part of the country and be confused. The actual reservations home are made either in my name or a fictitious name."

He doesn't limit escapes to major airlines. He'll also see if charter lines have flights out of the recovery area. Trains, buses, and boats, too, he checks.

"In one particular case, we were on an island, so I found some local charter boats," he said. "It was in St. Thomas, and when we got to the airport I realized there was no way out. Police were there with the original absconding parent. On those islands, you don't want to be detained. You could be there forever. We immediately turned around and drove down to the dock, called a particular charter boat captain and told him I had a party who wanted a scenic trip to St. Croix. Two hours later, we were on his boat, my client, the child, myself. My two men took back our rental cars and flew to New York."

Sometimes he won't come directly home. He'll take the first flight out of a recovery area, no matter where it goes. In major cities, of course, there are options—trains, buses, even the possibility of driving to another city.

Once he's found a child, he hires local investigators to watch the house where the child and the absconding parent live. "That saves two days," he said. "So when we get there, we know exactly what exists." The local men will have learned the routine of the absconding parent and tell Cerone when is the best time for recovery.

He likes to fly out of New York at night so he'll have a full day in the new state to draw his maps and plan his exit. The second day there he does the actual back-snatch, with the third day as a backup in case he might have to hide before leaving the area.

"In every case, though," he said, "I've been able to get out on that second day." He'll have his local men first send up pictures of the absconding parent's home, so he knows what it looks like before he leaves Great Neck. He plans the physical snatch in detail, too, with specific jobs for everyone.

"I sit with my client and tell her or him what to do," he said. "I tell them we work as a team. Everyone has a designated job. I instruct my client, 'When we get to a certain point, you will get out of the car. You will grab the child and return to the car. That is your sole function. You don't worry about anything else. Not fighting, kissing, or hugging, or anything else until you're in the car and we're on the road again.

"Then I tell her or him what each of *us* is going to do. I tell them on the plane going down and when we get there, I tell them again. The next morning I tell them again and five minutes before we're going to do it, I tell them yet again."

There are jobs for his two assistants, too.

"One man does nothing but drive," Cerone said. "A car is dumped driverless before the recovery, usually in a shopping center."

The driver has two jobs. He must know each escape route, and he must make sure all four doors of the car are unlocked. "Can you imagine trying to recover a kid and, in all that confusion, running back to the car and finding it is locked?" he asked. "It's happened. In that split second, you can lose the whole thing."

His second man is the strongest of his team, he claimed, muscular, trained in self-defense. "We are unarmed and may have to defend ourselves and our client," he said. This second man is a bodyguard who makes sure no punches are thrown, or, if they are thrown, he throws them.

"He'll get in the middle of a scuffle," Cerone said. "If he has to be left behind, he'll be left behind. Since we're acting in behalf of the client, hired by that client, there's no penalty he can suffer by staying there."

Most of his recoveries have been quiet and quick, he claimed. There was one that wasn't.

A mother and father separated, but were not divorced. No one had custody of their three-year-old boy, who stayed with his mom in Dix Hills on Long Island when his father went to San Francisco. The husband decided he wanted the child about two months later.

"Since it was an open custody thing, we decided we'd help him," Cerone said. "It was tough because we had to deal with a three-year-old who went to nursery school and lived in a very residential neighborhood. We staked out the house for two days before the husband flew in from the Coast.

"In the morning, all the mothers brought their kids out to the curb and waited for the school bus. Our client came in and we sat near the house the next morning. We had everything set up: second car, flights back to San Francisco. We sat there for the day and decided it wouldn't be in our interest to try and take the kid when he went to school. His mother stood out there with him until the bus came.

"We stayed there for two days, following the mother, hoping for the child to be on his own. But it was impossible; every place the kid went, the mother was with him."

He had to think of some other way to grab the boy. Usually, children are taken on weekday mornings while they wait for a school bus on a street corner. There are other kids around, but no parents. Cerone came up with a new plan, not just different escape routes and reservations on several airlines.

"We decided we would cause a diversion," Cerone said. "This was in September 1977, and the next morning myself and one of our female assistants walked casually up the street like husband and wife while the mother stood there with her child. We figured we'd try it once and see how it worked. We said 'Good morning' to her, told her we were new in the neighborhood, and asked questions about schools.

"She was very cooperative. We talked for about twenty minutes and she invited us in for coffee, told us all about the area. It was decided that the following morning we would do the same thing, to make it look legitimate.

"Again, we talked with that mother until the bus came. We decided we would do this a third time, only my client and another person from the agency would be parked up the street, out of sight. We told our people that when they saw us start talking with the mother they should pull the car to the head of the driveway, where the child would be standing. I would give a signal, get between mother and child, and give our people, with the husband, a chance to reach out and grab the boy.

"The next morning came and we had this on a fine time schedule, because the bus was there at exactly 8:05 A.M. Monday through Friday. The mother came out six minutes before it arrived each morning. So, on our day to recover the child, she showed up on time with the kid. My assistant and I went up the block and got to the driveway at the same time she did. Again, we talked with her and the child played with other children. My assistant and I stood directly between the child and the mother, who were about ten feet apart.

"I gave the signal, which was to put my hand on my head, and our pickup car, with the father in it, came down the street. What happened next was the most incredible thing I have ever seen in this business."

The bus was early, four minutes early. It came one way down the street and Cerone's car came from the *other* way. Both headed for the driveway, the bus's usual pickup spot for children on that block. "Both vehicles screeched brakes and met head-on, about six inches apart, right where that driveway met the street," he said. "The wife saw her husband jump out of the car and grab their son. I'm six foot tall and weigh two hundred twenty pounds and this woman, who couldn't have been more than one hundred ten or one hundred fifteen pounds, goes right over me. She knocked me down.

"Then we had to push and shove, push and shove. He's holding on to the kid. She's holding on to the kid. They are yelling and screaming and cursing at each other. I'm grabbing her and trying to pull her away from our car and telling her she could get hurt and she's yelling, 'They're kidnapping my son! They're kidnapping my son!'

"Meanwhile, the driver is getting off the bus with his two attendants. Other neighbors from up the street are all converging. This whole thing takes about thirty seconds and there were about twenty people standing there, watching. Finally, I am trying to pull the woman away and I rip off her dress, her *whole* dress. There she is with nothing on.

"Finally, our men got the kid in the car, backed up and took off. The woman is hysterical and yells, 'Get the plate number.' I ran out in the middle of the street like a good citizen and called out the wrong plate number, of course. Then my girl and I just faded out, walked slowly away. We went back to the drop site where the first car had been left. Drove it around for about an hour, returned it.

"There was one other thing. As we walked away, we saw squad cars with red lights flashing go toward the house. I found out later the police dropped out of it when they learned it was the husband who had the boy. What got me was that out of all those people at the scene, no one lifted a hand.

"I don't like them that way," Cerone said. "I don't like to be left behind, because I don't like to walk. It was very messy."

Cerone's office is on the first floor of an apartment building in Great Neck. There are four rooms, two secretaries, and about eighteen employees. Most of his agents investigate accident and insurance claims and divorces, where one spouse tries to prove the other is cheating.

There are bowling trophies around the office, movie posters on pine-paneled walls, plants on dusty windowsills. Cigar smoke hangs in the rooms. Cerone works in blue jeans, boots or sneakers, red or blue flannel shirts in winter.

He has a license to carry a gun, but never takes it with him. There was a time, however, when he might have used it, because an angry father attacked him with a shotgun. Cerone chose to flee, however, rather than fight. It was a case different from most of his others because he did his homework, but couldn't recover the child. The reason: The abductor had been tipped off that Cerone and a victimized mother were coming.

A New York City mother hired him in August 1977, to find and recover her six-year-old son. She and her husband had been divorced about six months. Cerone found the boy and his father in Fort Lauderdale, Florida, two months later. He had a local investigator watch the house, and learned the man left every morning on his motorcycle at 7:30 A.M. The boy came out at 8:10 A.M. to get on the school bus. He was alone on a street corner, waiting by himself.

"I thought it would be damn easy," Cerone said. "We went down to Florida the night before and got to the house about seven o'clock the next morning. Our intention was that no matter how good the chance, we wouldn't take the child at this time. I wanted to see with my own two eyes what the situation was.

"Sure enough, at seven-thirty out came the father. At exactly eight-ten, the boy walks out to the street corner and the bus picks him up. We decided that tomorrow morning, we would do it."

But they didn't. Cerone was almost killed.

"Next morning, we showed up at seven o'clock again. But the boy didn't go to the school bus." Cerone staked out the house for another half hour.

"Then I went up and knocked on the door. It opened and there was the boy," Cerone said. "I said, 'Hi, son, how are you? Can I speak with your father?' "

Cerone felt there was something wrong. The child was nervous and wouldn't stand still. "I looked past him and there is the father," he said. "He came out from the shadows and opened the screen door and pointed a twelve-gauge shotgun between my eyes. He said, 'If you think you or that wife of mine is going to get this kid back, you got another thing coming.' "

The man stood over six feet tall and was about thirty years old. He also weighed about 275 pounds, Cerone thought.

"At this point, I started to walk away and when I was about fifteen feet away and heard him start to pull the trigger, I decided it was time to run, and run fast," he said. "I remembered everything I learned in the army. Zig-zag. Sure enough, he let go both barrels. Fortunately for me, I'm alive to talk about it."

He couldn't figure out what went wrong and stayed in Fort Lauderdale two more days. But the child was never out of his father's reach. They thought of charging the man with attempted murder, assault, or unlawful discharge of a weapon. They also considered going to civil court to have Florida enforce the mother's New York custody order, which Florida is supposed to do, but sometimes doesn't.

Back in New York, Cerone went over the woman's case. Did she tell anyone what she was doing? "She said the only person she had told was her deepest confidant, a girl she had known since childhood. They had grown up together and had been friends for twenty-eight years," he said. This friend had even loaned her money for plane fare, she told him.

Cerone was suspicious. He learned where this friend lived and checked her phone bills. For the last six months, he learned, this "friend" had called the woman's ex-husband nearly every day. He then checked the man's number in Fort Lauderdale and "Lo and behold, there was a ton of them [calls] to my client's 'friend' in New York," he said.

"I found out later that this girlfriend had been having an affair with the husband all these years," he said.

The former husband called up his ex-wife for several weeks after her aborted recovery. He didn't send money and said she'd never see her son again. Cerone tried a new tack.

"I put a lot of pressure on him," he said. "Financial pressure. I spoke to his employer and spread vicious rumors about him. Basically, I told people what he had done. I found out which companies he dealt with. He was an auto mechanic and I told his neighbors, too. Three months later he brought back his child, claiming he couldn't find work."

The woman moved to upstate New York, where she now works as a sports instructor, allows her ex-husband to visit with the boy, and said the child is doing well in school.

Cerone checks out his clients before making a recovery, he said. "If I feel that my client is not stable enough or doesn't have the right papers, or even the right motivation, I won't take the case, even if the person has custody.

"For instance, if I know the father was successful and the mother a convicted drug addict, prostitute or child neglector, I wouldn't touch it, even if the courts had given her custody. I would find the child, perhaps, but she'd have to pursue it through the courts.

"If my client is a man, I do the same thing," he explained.

"Check around, dig into his past. Maybe he never cared for his children while he was married and just wants to harass his ex-wife. I've turned down fathers like that."

Cerone also wants to see if his client is stable and tries to figure out if he or she would be a good parent. He'll ask a person to come back for a second interview and try to have a long conversation with him or her. They'll talk about different subjects and Cerone will attempt to form a character profile of the person. Then he'll decide whether or not to take the case.

14

Children: The Emotional Impact

In the midst of it all are the children. The effects on them can be devastating. Some children eventually learn to accept the experience, but many carry lifelong scars. Almost always, children go through a difficult period of readjustment in the weeks and months following the recovery.

Most abducted children return home unstable, afraid of being alone. They cling to loved ones and fear strangers, doorbells, telephones. Some parents find their children have been neglected. While gone, they weren't taken care of properly, lacked medical treatment, or may not have had a parent with them at all. Some children are in poor health when brought home and need physical as well as emotional support.

Leonard Pauser, forty-one, a New York City policeman living in suburban Westchester County, waited for his two children to return from a Sunday visit with his ex-wife two years ago. Pauser had custody of them—a son, ten, and a daughter, three. He waited all night.

The boy came home a week later, but it took Pauser ten months to track his ex-wife and daughter to Florida, the Caribbean, and finally back to her apartment in Manhattan. He said that when he got his daughter home she was seriously underweight. His ex-wife was broke and was wanted for welfare fraud.

"She was in a very debilitated state," he said of his daughter. "She was very tall for three years old and weighed only twenty-eight pounds. Now she's on a good diet with vitamins, and is up to thirty-two pounds."

Len Pauser's little girl wanted to be at his side, always. "I let her cling to me and she literally followed me everywhere I went," he said. "That went on for several weeks, but I felt she needed me and just tried to wean her a little bit at a time. If we have friends in the house, she is very timid and shy. She will not go near strangers or have anything to do with them."

Because of his job, he couldn't stay home every day, and so he put his daughter in day care. She became upset if he didn't pick her up himself.

"If it's not me who takes her and picks her up, she cries, even if it's someone she knows and likes. It's always, 'Daddy, are you going to come for me before dark time?' If it's four thirty or five o'clock and she doesn't see me, she gets very upset.

"At night we go through all kinds of rituals, like leaving the door open and the lights on and am I going to be right there all the time? Every night she worries that I'm going to go out and leave her alone," he explained.

"She still has that thing in the back of her mind," Pauser said. "She doesn't like my new wife and I to go anyplace and leave her. There's no such thing as baby-sitters."

There was also a problem with his daughter going to sleep at night. "She never had nightmares, but she did have trouble getting to sleep," he said. "Now she's in a pattern and knows that at eight o'clock she's in bed. In the beginning, she'd have her bath and be in her pajamas and say her prayers and then want me to stay with her until she went to sleep. That was a problem, especially when I had to work nights, but little by little she has come to accept that at eight o'clock she's in bed and has to go to sleep."

Another parent who recovered her child found a similar reaction in her son.

Carol Zenith, thirty-six, is an attorney in Manhattan. She was married for seven years to a salesman, Gino, forty-one, who represents a manufacturing firm in Italy. The couple has one child, a son, Daniel, who is now nine years old. When they divorced, they agreed Carol would have custody.

But several years ago, in January, Daniel vanished on his way home from school. His father called a day later from Rome and said, "I have my son. Be careful what you tell him. Don't say anything that is going to upset him."

Carol agrees that children, once recovered, need very special attention from the parent. She said the situation with her son, who was returned four months later after a bitter court suit in Rome, was tense.

"I couldn't go to work," she said. "I tried to take him with me, but I couldn't take him to the office every day, so most of the time I just stayed home, for the first three or four months. Then I had to take him to a psychiatrist a number of times.

"Literally, he wouldn't let me walk into another room. He would look under the bed at night before he went to sleep, and he had to sleep in the same bed with me. I would look under the bed, too, and then we would check to see that the windows were closed and the door was locked. The doctor said I had better let him sleep in the bed with me as it would take him a year to get over this.

"Daniel couldn't verbalize why he was scared, couldn't make sense of it. It was like an obsession. If the phone rang and I went to the other room, he would get out of bed and come and stand with me."

It took about a year for young Daniel to adjust, to be able to speak of his abduction. "It was the strangest thing," Carol said, "because just about a year afterward he suddenly told me about the plane trip over. Until then if I or anybody mentioned that trip at all, he just didn't remember anything.

"He told me how he was scared and how he fought with his father and was crying and his father forced him on the plane and he threw up. I thought maybe he'd gone willingly. He loves his father. But I think it was panic for him. After all, he had lived with me all of his life and knew his father as a visitor and was just too young to cope with being separated from me.

"I know it was a very tough thing for him. It's very hard for a child to say, 'I was scared because I was with my father.' I don't think his father told him, until he got out to the airport, where they were going."

Carol sends her son to Italy now at least twice a year to see his father. She told how she tried to train him to reach her if something happened. "Please God, it is over now, but each Christmas when Daniel goes for a visit, I get nervous. Daniel is at the point now where he can make a phone call. I'm teaching him to call from Italy and how to get to the American Embassy. When he was taken, he had no concept of time. He couldn't write or mail a letter and that made him helpless.

"Child stealing usually happens to the young child," she said, "because they are helpless and have to cling to whichever parent is there. He lived with his grandparents over there and clung to his grandfather because he was the only person he had, the only constant that he had for four months. When he came home, he would eat and then throw up. He wouldn't stay with my father, who he loved dearly. Certainly not with a housekeeper or a baby-sitter; absolutely not."

Parents learn to live with their child's fear. They set aside time to be alone with their son or daughter, adjust their lives to fit their child's needs. They want to reassure the child of their love, and try to counter any attempts of their ex-spouse to brainwash the child.

One Chicago mother recovered her five-year-old son from Dallas, Texas, with the help of a vigilante. They picked up her boy after following him and his father to a shopping center, and were able to lose themselves in the crowd after the recovery.

The woman, an advertising copywriter, was able to take work home. Kindergarten was only half a day and she'd go to her office when her son was in school, pick him up every noon, and bring his toys to her workroom at home. She felt he'd been taught to hate her, and also to hate her job, during the seven months he lived with his father.

"You could call it brainwashing, I guess," the mother, Elena Hoffman, thirty-one, said. "It wasn't anything you could notice directly. But every now or then he'd say something like, 'Mommy likes her work more than me,' or 'Why do you have to use the typewriter when I'm here?'

"I think he'd been taught to say that by his father, who worked on his own father's ranch and lived with a woman who stayed home," she said. "In fact, my son even complained once that I wasn't doing enough housework. He'd found dirty dishes in the sink."

John Raleigh, the vigilante quoted earlier, feels that the short-term trauma recovering a child might create is worth risking because it removes the child from the much more damaging influence of the absconding parent. "Taking back kids *doesn't* hurt them," he said, "but the original abduction does. Every recovery I've been involved with hasn't had any damaging effect on the children. But what *does* have a bad influence is what some of these absconding parents say to their children."

He described what some parents on the run tell their children. "A man in Tennessee told his girls their mother didn't love them and didn't want them. We've had a lot of them say the other parent is dead. That's *much* more damaging than an actual recovery. Some kids may go through a few moments where they are startled during the recovery, but by the time we get them in the car, within a minute or two they settle right down and there is no problem."

There was a case where an absconding mother had told her son to run if he saw his father again, because the man would beat him. "I helped a Michigan father get his boy back from Iowa," Raleigh said. "The mother had told the child that his father, if he took him home, wouldn't feed him and would lock him in a closet. That poor boy ran when he first saw his father and put up a little struggle. Now he's okay."

Raleigh said that since the boy came home he'd had calls from his mother, asking him where he wanted to live. "You shouldn't put a child in a position like that," he said. "The boy wouldn't give her an answer for fear of hurting her. So the mother said, 'Well, you can sit there and rot in hell with your father.' "

Perhaps the most immediate damage done to stolen children is that they miss school. Parents first worry about emotional problems, but they soon realize their children must begin normal lives, which means going to class. Yet because of sudden, prolonged absences, some of these stolen children might have to repeat a year, which may cause more problems.

Harry Casson, for instance, the California father mentioned in Chapter 8 whose boy was taken to Ohio, felt his son missed too much classwork. "When he came back he had regressed," Casson said. "He was tested and was in the twenty-eighth percentile at school. He'd missed so much work, nearly eight months. Whereas when he left, he was in the eightieth percentile. They [his former wife and her boyfriend] had never put him in school while he was away."

Because of special tutoring, the boy wasn't put back a grade. Casson's second wife was a teacher and she had colleagues who volunteered their time. "Now he's pretty close to being back to snuff," Casson said. "But we couldn't have done it without my new wife. All that time my son was gone he wasn't in school. He just watched television and goofed around. He was like a vegetable," he said.

Casson blamed his son's absence from school on a judge in Ohio, who, as soon as Casson found the boy, put him in a home for runaway children. "He was there about two and a half months with kids who were runaways and delinquents. It was crazy. He was twenty-five hundred miles from home and in a strange place where he didn't know any of the kids and didn't know what was going to happen."

Casson wasn't even allowed to know where his boy was. "It was a specific female judge who didn't like men and wanted to prove her own thing. She was power hungry. She put him in a children's receiving center and then in a foster home for six weeks and never let me write to him. She wouldn't let me know his condition, even."

Harry Casson, with his family reconstructed, also spoke of his little boy's fear of being taken again. "Every so often things come out that indicate he still has a fear that he will be taken again," he said. "Yet he's embarrassed to talk about it. He doesn't want other kids to know. It's a scar. He wanted a big dog for protection, so we got him one."

Private investigator George Cerone has seen abducted children who've been neglected, brainwashed, and have had to live at a lower standard than they did before they were stolen. And the longer the children were gone, the more they show the effects.

"The majority of children I've brought back after, say, three months to a year are lighter in weight, pale, withdrawn. I usually talk with the custodial parent afterward, and he or she will say, 'The child's lost weight, is very quiet, has nightmares, fears airplanes, fears being left alone, and has trouble sleeping.'

"I just finished a case. It was a boy, and I had a chance to speak with him after we got him back. This is a boy who had always been in bed by eight o'clock at night and he told me that after his father snatched him, he had trouble sleeping. The father gave him NyQuil, the cold medicine, every night, and if that didn't [put him to sleep] he gave him Sudafed, [a decongestant] to make him drowsy. Of course, the fact that the father took him out every night to bars didn't help. He kept him out until three in the morning and got him up for school. This went on for two months. The boy was eight years old."

Cerone said that some children are afraid of men when they come home. "It's an absolute fear," he said. "I can't understand it. When I recover a child, I buy a toy, just as a token. But a lot of them won't take it. It's almost as if they think I'm trying to buy their affection.

Like Raleigh, Cerone agreed that recovering a child is not traumatic and that the main damage to abducted children can be brainwashing.

"The authority of the parent usually takes over," he said. "He or she picks up the child and they are happy. Children may cry for a few minutes until they realize what is happening. After that, it's kisses and hugs."

But there have been several times when Cerone found a child unwilling to be taken back. One girl was taken by her father when she was three. When she was recovered she was about five, and she balked. She'd grown to know her father's girlfriend as her mother and when the natural mother confronted her, she didn't know what to think. She'd been calling the girlfriend "Mommy."

"It took her a few days to realize and remember who her mother was. She was told her natural mother had died in an automobile accident and that she would now have the girlfriend as her mother. The child accepted this."

How did she adjust? "It took her grandmother," Cerone said. "Her father had never said anything about her grandmother, so she knew she could trust her grandmother. It was sad. When she was first recovered, she called for 'Mommy,' but it was for her surrogate mother."

Cerone said the child was under psychological evaluation for about three months once home.

The combination of fear—the thought of never going home again—and the gradual influence of the abducting parent contribute to making children lose self-confidence and to mistrust people around them.

Dr. Jeanette Minkoff, Probation Family Services co-ordinator of Monroe County, New York, has dealt with more than one hundred cases of parental kidnapping. Minkoff holds a doctorate in clinical psychology and has been with the county's probation department in Rochester, New York, for twelve years.

"Children have described their fears, sadness, loneliness, and hysteria upon realizing they were not being returned to their homes," she said. "Children have told me they begged, pleaded, and cried in an unsuccessful effort to persuade the kidnapping parent to return them. They know almost immediately that they have been lied to and sense the parent is in violation of the law.

"Children have stated their concern and worry about the other parent and sense the agonizing terror the other parent would feel when they were not returned.

"The kidnapping parent often explains to the child that he took him or her because he loves them so much, and children begin to wonder about love—'Do people have to hurt someone to love someone?' That's a direct quote from a six-year-old boy," she said.

Minkoff spoke of another difficult psychological trauma: being told to change their names. "A seven-year-old child told me he could not remember his new name or the falsified name of the school he was instructed to say he had last attended," she said. "He explained he did a lot of erasing on his papers, as he continued to write his own name.

"Another child told me she begged to call her other parent on her birthday, as she missed the parent terribly and knew if she were home there would be a party.

"A little boy, age five, told me his 'taking parent' did not have much money and they had to get clothes and shoes for him from a 'big box on the street.'

"All of these children were told by the kidnapping parent they would adjust and be happy soon. Unfortunately, none of them ever reached this promised plateau," she said.

Being told they will adjust soon and be happy—*without* the other parent—is how children come to be turned against the parent from whom they were stolen. They often begin to hate that parent, as one mother in California learned.

"In September 1975, my children, ages seven, nine, and ten, were spirited away from their school and my custody to the state of Washington. For the past years, I have struggled through the confounding maze of the courts," she said.

It took Washington three years to decide she could have custody. But her ex-husband, a lawyer, tried to have his new wife adopt the children, and that battle took another year.

She finally saw her children for the first time in four years at her lawyer's office in Spokane, Washington.

"What has been done to my children is truly beyond belief," she said. "They have become robots and frightening examples of the most horrific form of child abuse.

"Since September 1975, my children have been told and led to believe that I don't love them or want them.

"They have been told that I have made no effort to see them, write them, or send them anything; that all my efforts were directed at trying to make the family unhappy," she said.

"They have been taught to hate me, taught to deny their belief in God and deny their Catholic upbringing, with such statements as 'Believing in God and Jesus is like believing in fairy tales, something that not very bright people believe.' They espouse such statements as, 'You were our biological carrier, but you are not our mother.' They are concerned about denying any part of themselves that indicates any relationship to me.

"My oldest daughter says, 'There's a part of you in me, and I hate that part.'

"My Christmas presents for December 1978, were at my attorney's office, and when he tried to give them the gifts, the children shouted, 'We don't want anything from her. She can't buy us,' " the mother said.

She said how she'd sent birthday presents for her daughter's thirteenth birthday, but they'd been returned, too. She even bought an ad in a local newspaper wishing her daughter well. Her children shouted at her during their brief visit, said they hated her.

"They screamed to get away and out of the office. They would not allow me to speak, nor would they sit or stop pacing. The terror, panic, and fear they exhibited was incomprehensible."

Children who are stolen often lose their ability to trust others. They feel insecure, unloved, angry at the parent left behind for not coming to see them, resentful at the absconding parent for uprooting them. They also feel guilty. Maybe they caused their parents to divorce.

Peg Edwards, thirty-two, a licensed clinical social worker in Santa Ana, California, has a private practice in family therapy and marriage counseling. In 1978 she saw her first child who'd been stolen and recovered. Since then she's seen about fifty other children.

"Their biggest problem is the fear that when they grow up they won't form healthy relationships," Edwards believes. "They lack trust and security, and this lack can cause them to behave poorly in school."

She points out that stolen children differ from other children in divorce because they haven't seen one parent for some time, perhaps even years. "Often they are taken when very young," Edwards said, "which is a crucial time in their development. It's a time when parents are the main figures in their lives, the people whom they are most likely to trust. If that trust is broken, the child becomes confused."

Such confusion can lead to guilt and anger. "We usually see children with a great sense of guilt," Edwards said. "They feel they were to blame. Maybe they did something to cause the divorce or didn't behave properly and that's why they were taken. 'Well, I wasn't a good boy (or good girl) and that's why Mommy or Daddy let me go.' They don't know why they're stolen. All they see is that perhaps they were bad and that's why Mommy or Daddy let them go and doesn't come after them.

"There are a lot of children questioning that. They have a lack of trust and belief in their parents. They had *two* parents, now they have one, and they don't know why. This is confusing and traumatic for the parent who has lost them, too, because when these children come home they can be angry, asking why the victimized parent didn't come see them."

Anger makes it hard for parents to adjust. "There's one mother I'm working with who just got her two little girls back after a year," Edwards said. "They are five years old and three years old, and initially the five-year-old slapped her mother, kicked her, wouldn't call her 'Mom,' only used her first name and said things like, 'You didn't care about me. Why do you want me now? Daddy cares about me.'

"This child was brainwashed by her father while she was gone. She's been in treatment for about three months. Now she calls her mother 'Mom' and is beginning to express her anger more appropriately. She's beginning to understand. Last week she came in and said, 'I just found out that it wasn't because Mommy didn't love me that she didn't see me. She couldn't *find* me. I didn't know that. If only I could have called her and told her where I was.'

"At the time she was stolen she felt her mother didn't want her. That's what her father had told her," Edwards said.

Stolen children undergo such severe trauma, she points out, that to them it's like one parent has died. "It's a total loss to them," she said. "They have no awareness of life or death at that young age. That's why there's so much confusion when they come home. They think, 'I thought my mommy or daddy was completely gone.' They say, 'Where have you been all the time I was suffering?'

"It's a lot harder on a child, in fact, than a real death. In an actual death, the other parent is their support and would have experienced the loss, too. But in child snatching, the child has no way of talking about it. The abducting parent doesn't want to talk about it, which alienates the child even more from that absent parent," she said.

Families come together when someone dies. Relatives fly in from other states. They support each other. Children see uncles, aunts, cousins. They know they belong. Stolen children see practically no one. There are no reunions and family dinners, no offers of help. There is just hiding. When they come home, they may have to hide again. Everyone fears a second kidnapping.

Edwards sees the children once a week and keeps in touch with the parent who recovered them. "Some children are still very fearful," she said. "It works both ways. The parent who stole them doesn't want them to be outside and then the parent who gets them back *also* is frightened. They don't want their children going to school. They're afraid if they play in the schoolyard on recess they may be restolen."

She advises parents to let schools know what has happened, to have teachers look for strangers outside playgrounds. She tells children to report anyone new watching their house or school. And she tries to help both parents and children start new lives.

"There's a lot of new parenting skills to learn," Edwards said. "It can be like building a whole new relationship. Children taken at a very young age, say at two or three, might not remember that victimized parent, especially if there was a girlfriend or boyfriend with the absconding parent while on the run."

How does she treat recovered children? What does she tell them and their parents? With children, she has them express themselves. "I have them draw and play with clay," she said. "They play with dollhouses and act out their fantasies. If there is an intense feeling, they don't show it directly. When you ask them to draw their mom or dad, they may draw blank faces. I try to build a sense of trust in them, a sense of security, a place where they can express their feelings.

"They come into a play therapy room, where they can draw or whatever. I let them know that I'm someone who isn't going to tell them what's right or wrong, in a certain sense, about their parents. They're used to being with one parent. Perhaps that parent has said, 'Don't talk about your mother (or father), she (or he) is bad.' Neither parent is all bad and neither parent is all good. But I have to have the child realize there is a balance and that he or she can talk to me about it.

"I'm here to help them express their confusion, make sense out of it and be someone they can talk to. I see children for about six months, on an average."

She speaks with parents about every two weeks and urges them to become parents again. She feels children need discipline as well as love. Parents want to show that they love their recovered children, but sometimes can't be strict. But too much freedom can also hurt a child. "Just because you've missed a child for a year doesn't mean that you are going to let them walk all over you," Edwards said. "Most of these adults aren't acting like parents. It's hard for them. They want to make up for that lost time."

Edwards spoke of "a five-year-old who kicked and slapped her mother, for instance. I told the mother, 'Don't just yell at the child, but don't ignore the hitting. Don't allow it. Take

the child, at that moment, sit down and help her to understand that her feelings are okay. She's angry. Don't make her
feel she has to hide it.' "

Edwards lets parents know how their children are doing
and tells them when to set limits. Children react to discipline differently. "Usually, there is anger," she said. "But
sometimes children will withdraw into depression and won't
express any emotion."

By dealing with their anger, depression, and guilt, Edwards works to build trust, to make children feel they are
worthy.

"When a child comes back, he or she has a lack of confi-
dence," Edwards said. "Basically that comes from not knowing where they stand, from all those questions that have
come up while he or she was away. If children feel loved,
they'll be confident and secure. If there are those questions:
'What happened to me? Am I *really* loved? Is someone going
to protect me?' they will still be off-balance."

Parents need to keep their children away from hassles,
away from bitterness about money, away from spite. She
encourages parents to let their recovered children talk with
and see their other parent. She suggests supervised visitation, where the abductor can visit his or her children without the danger of taking them again, usually coming to the
home of the parent who now has the child.

Edwards has talked with parents who have stolen children, too, and feels that some of them may well have taken
them out of love. "You see a lot of anger and hostility toward
the opposing parent," she said. "But you see a lot of love for
the children, too." Edwards thinks that fathers, especially,
may feel left out of the custody process. "In many cases," she
said, "a father was frustrated in court and didn't feel he
could win. He thought he was the better parent. This was
his reason for snatching."

A parent's fear of losing his or her children, of never seeing them again, makes *children* afraid, too. Parents who re-

cover them sometimes won't even let their kids answer the phone. They're afraid for them to have *any* contact with the other parent.

"Some parents don't put their preschool children in nursery schools or day care," Edwards said. "They don't want them located. They won't even let them play outside with neighborhood children. A child can't feel safe and secure in that kind of environment."

15

Children:
The Long-term Effects

Stolen children carry scars from their abductions which last many years. One California woman didn't learn her real name until she was twenty-five years old.

Lorraine Kannon is divorced and has a daughter, thirteen, and a son, ten. Now thirty, she was stolen by her mother when she was seven years old. She hasn't seen her father since.

"I didn't know my last name for a long time because it was changed five or six times," she said. "Every time my mother had a new boyfriend, I had to use that name when I went to school."

She ran away from home when she was fifteen. "There was a lot of friction between my mother and I because I wanted the truth and she wouldn't talk to me," she said. "I remembered my father, but wasn't allowed to talk about him. I haven't seen him since I was seven, and that was in Indianapolis. He came over once and my mother said if she ever saw him again she'd put him in jail."

Her mother moved a lot: to Florida, Ohio, New York, Washington State, finally California, always using different names. Kannon's oldest brother left home when she was fourteen and she missed him. But her mother said, "Oh, he's not your brother. I didn't really have him."

"There was another kick in the head," Kannon said, "and I didn't know what was going on. I got so I didn't trust *anyone*. I didn't trust my mother. She lied constantly. I remember loving my father and she wanted to put him in jail."

So she ran away, stayed with friends, took drugs, drank. Another brother, who was thirteen then, went with her. They slept in abandoned buildings, stole food from stores, took clothes from Goodwill barrels. They began by staying in a friend's garage, then went to other friends, and on to parks, meadows, beaches. They hitched rides in California and headed for Indiana, where they hoped to find their father.

But California police found them. "Mom came down to the jail," Kannon said, "and told us our father had died in a car accident."

Kannon ran away again. "We never had any affection in our house from my mother and I started looking for affection from men and ended up in bad situations."

She went to Venice, California, where she met other runaways. Some of them were also looking for missing parents. It was 1965, just before flower children blossomed in San Francisco. She tried LSD and sex, then married at sixteen and had two children before she was twenty years old.

"I married too young because I wanted a family," she said. "I wanted to belong. The first man who said he loved me, married me. I had no goals, except to be loved. But I confused love with sex and wasn't ready to have a family. Yet I wanted a child to love, so that I would have someone who could never be taken away from me."

In 1970 she was divorced. Somehow she coped. Somehow she pulled through, survived. It wasn't easy. "The divorce was the best thing to happen to me," she said. "But not right away. Right away I got back into drugs, overdosed, and wound up in a hospital and didn't know how I got there.

"Then I saw a psychologist, went to school, pulled myself together. I'm going back to college again," she said.

Kannon's off welfare and works as a secretary. She wants

to study advertising. Her professional life is coming together. But her personal life still shakes.

"I'm engaged now and can't imagine having one long-term relationship. I'm scared, absolutely. It's what I want with all my heart. Yet, I don't know how to deal with it. I'm afraid of losing someone again. I've broken up with three men because I was afraid of losing them and was scared they would leave. So, I cut off those relationships. Now I'm trying again."

Lorraine Kannon and her new fiancé have gone for therapy. She wants to overcome her fear and thinks that with proper counseling she can succeed. There is still her father to find, however, and herself to trust. She's building self-confidence.

"I always had a lack of identity," she said. "A total lack of self-worth. When you're young, you go through this questioning, this 'Who *am* I, anyway?' thing. I went through it severely and couldn't remember things and had mental blocks. I didn't know fantasy from reality for a while, even while I was an adult and worked as a secretary. I went to a psychologist for three years before I could tell what was real, and how that was different from what I was told.

"When I was twenty-seven, I sat in the office one day and started to cry, for no reason. That's when I started therapy."

She didn't trust anyone, didn't respect herself. She felt guilty, too, that she had created her confusion, resented what had happened to her, and was afraid that if she found her father he wouldn't want her. It was too much to handle at times.

"I have scars on my wrist from when I tried to kill myself when I was eight years old," she said. "I just felt so unloved, and went to church one day and heard about God and love, and I thought, That's where I want to be. I wanted to go where He was and locked myself in the bathroom with a razor."

Lorraine Kannon didn't discover her real name until 1979.

She had lived with foster parents in Indiana for a while, just after she'd tried to kill herself. She remembered them and they looked up her birth certificate in Indianapolis. It was Lorraine Joi. When her children were born, she'd put her wrong maiden name on their certificates.

It made her angry. "Any parent who steals a child is going to be rejected by that child, eventually," she said. Kannon hasn't seen her mother in thirteen years.

Some children aren't as lucky as Lorraine Kannon. They don't find themselves, never settle, drift in and out of mental hospitals, live on welfare. Many women who had been abducted themselves as children, have children who end up in foster homes. Often men of a similar background can't hold jobs, drink heavily, become criminals. All are angry, resentful, defensive, searching. As children they needed to know who they were, whom they could trust, if they were worthy. As adults, they have the same questions.

Dr. Simon Tauberg, a psychiatrist in Miami, Florida, has worked with stolen children who grew into "stolen" adults. A transplanted New Yorker, Tauberg has a private practice, but has also worked with the Dade County Probation Department and its counselors for many years. Some of the people he's talked to who have had trouble with the law were stolen as children. All grew up knowing only one parent, who abandoned them to relatives years after they were stolen.

"As adults they have the same problems as when they were young," Tauberg said. "Only their emotional stress is more pronounced. Their fears, lack of self-confidence have grown, not diminished, over the years. They are antisocial, and can be more destructive now than angry children. Instead of breaking toys or throwing temper fits, they will get drunk or start fights, shoplift or use drugs. They feel cheated. Life didn't give them a chance, they feel. Society didn't reach out. There are no clinics for stolen children, no

Alcoholics Anonymous–type groups for child-stealing victims. No therapy centers."

It's a problem that society has neglected, Tauberg feels. Parents who've lost children have no place to turn. Neither do their children, especially when they grow up.

"It's the children who need therapy the most," Tauberg said. "They've grown up with confusion and doubt, with so many unanswered questions, with no roots, so to speak."

Tauberg spoke of Estelle Thackery, thirty-two, who was picked up in Miami Beach for stealing costume jewelry from a department store. She'd been arrested before for prostitution and petty larceny.

"The woman told me she'd been taken by her father from Boston as a six-year-old," Tauberg said. "She'd lived in six states, mainly with cousins in Philadelphia, Pennsylvania, but also in Ohio. Then it was two foster homes and one reform school. Again the charge was shoplifting. She did it to get attention."

Thackery was bitter, Tauberg said. She'd had no children. But there'd been three abortions and now she couldn't conceive, which made her *more* angry. "She wanted a home," he said, "wanted to get married, adopt children. But she felt used, thrown away. Life was cheap thrills, quick money. She'd worked as a topless dancer, cocktail waitress, but couldn't get straightened out. Now she's in therapy, doing well. Her probation officer feels she has more than a fifty-fifty chance of becoming useful and happy."

Another woman who, like Lorraine Kannon and Estelle Thackery, was stolen as a child agrees with Dr. Tauberg. She, too, grew up questioning herself. But she was able to find herself before it was too late.

Doris Freeman, thirty-seven, is a professor of English at a university near Washington, D.C. As a four-year-old she lived with her parents in southern California. One night she was taken by her father and driven to Florida. This experi-

ence made her distrust people. She grew up shy and withdrawn, doing well in school, but with few friends. She was
passive as a child and as an adolescent; she looked upon
herself as a victim.

"My parents were in a situation where they were isolated
from any relatives," she said, "and the marriage started to
disintegrate because of the war and being away from any
home ties. My mother went away and left me with my father. This was all agreed upon and she was supposed to be
taking a nurse's training course.

"My father took me to visit my mother a month or two
after she had left home, and while we were there I was
upstairs playing with some other children. He called me to
come down and I couldn't because I was in the bathroom.
When I *did* come down, I saw he was gone. Apparently they
had argued and she had called the police and he had left.

"About two days later, he came back with a large box
filled with clothes, set it down on the kitchen table and said
that he had decided little girls should stay with their mothers. My mother was very happy and pleased and she relaxed
at that moment. He went to the door and said to me, 'Aren't
you going to kiss me good-bye?'

"I ran into his open arms and he snatched me and raced to
the car, which was running all the time. She ran after him
and held on to the back of the car and he dragged her for
half a block and all I could see was my mother, bloody. Even
now, it is difficult to talk about. He kept driving for three
days straight, to Florida, where *his* mother and relatives
were.

"I do remember what I said to my father. I screamed
when he threw me into the car and I said I wished I was
grown up, so that I could do something.

"I didn't see my mother again until I was twenty-one."

Even today, Doris Freeman remembers their ride.

"Thinking back on it," she said, "I realize that on that
drive across country with my father, I wished I was dead. I

sat in the bottom of the car and didn't say a word, at least that first day. I just wanted to reach out and destroy. It was anger, of course, and I was immobile with fear. Later, I became very passive and, of course, got good responses from people because I was so passive.

"Then I grew up being told that my mother was an awful person. Yet I knew that wasn't the whole picture, because I remembered her as a very loving and warm person. To me she was a good mother, and yet here I was hearing all these things which contradicted that."

Doris had to live with conflict, she explained, in that she liked her father, who was a salesman and outgoing, yet questioned his stealing her. And she wondered why her mother didn't call.

"I not only had some bad feelings about my father, in respect to what had happened, but there was the feeling of 'Why didn't she do something?'" Doris said. "I remember that she had called once and there was a big fuss. My father's family was politically important in Florida and they had a good deal of money and she knew if she came there, they would pass me from one relative to another."

Her sudden trip to Florida and not being able to see her mother changed her.

"I was a very happy and healthy child up until that point," she said. "From pictures of me and the way people who knew me as a child talk, I was a happy little kid. At the time, we lived near Hollywood. My parents had me with them and they were watching a movie being filmed and the director came over and said, 'Who is this little girl?' He put them in touch with acting lessons and things of that sort and I was given an award at the Child Actors gathering. I have it pasted in my baby book. It was an award for personality and outgoingness and that I was one of the most promising child actors at that time. I remember it happening in the Hollywood Bowl, and have good memories of those times," she said.

"But when we went to Florida, I was studious, quiet, a good little girl. School was a refuge, my way of getting away from having to relate to the real people in my life. I was fearful of getting close to anybody again, you know, to be openhearted with anyone, because after running to my father to kiss him good-bye and being so deeply betrayed, it spoiled something that had been between us.

"Also, emotionally, I was closer to my mother, as little girls would tend to be at that age, I suppose. I knew that my father loved me, but he was taking me away from my mother, who loved me, too. I felt I was under the complete control of someone who was capable of doing this horrible thing."

Her loneliness grew as she did. "As a teenager, I had a difficult time making close friends. I didn't date until college," Doris said. "I simply found it difficult to develop closeness in any relationship.

"There were other factors involved. My father was a salesman and changed jobs a good deal. We moved around frequently while I was growing up. There were also a couple of boarding schools, so it was just a pattern that developed.

"Then my father remarried and I didn't get along all that well with my stepmother. I fought with her because I resented the fact that she was not my real mother. Yet I was afraid to tell anybody that I *did* have a real mother. They pretended for years that I was her real child."

Doris felt her father and stepmother didn't realize what she went through. "My stepmother would have helped if she had known what I had gone through. I recognized she was a good woman and was doing all she could. But my father met her after all this had happened and convinced her my mother was some kind of slut, that it would be contaminating for me to be around her.

"She was much younger than he and I think she came to realize something was wrong. Yet he simply wouldn't talk about it."

Doris Freeman carried her abduction inside her, along with her distrust of people. It kept her from developing deep friendships and affected her first marriage.

"I did not mention to anybody what had happened to me," she said, "until at least five years after my father stole me. I would never talk about it. Up until recently, I could only mention it to people who I would come close to. I had friends along the way, but there was never any feeling that it could be ongoing or that relationships could last through the years. It was as though everything was always going to be disrupted, or cut off in some kind of violent way.

"I married at twenty-two, but I was really socially and emotionally very immature. I picked someone I couldn't trust, so it was just one disastrous thing after another in my marriage. He was seven years older than I and had problems of his own.

"It wasn't that I picked out people who did disastrous things, but there was a self-destructive element going on. I married the first chance I got. Something in me was blind in terms of knowing how to relate to people at that point. The marriage was disastrous for ten years, but in spite of that I went ahead and got my Ph.D.

"Then the marriage broke up and I sat down and decided I had to do something with my life to create stability, to let myself be, and to open up; and I began to take steps to do so, and I think my life is very good now. In fact, I am getting married soon. I was separated and divorced in 1973 and was about two months into analysis at that point. I'd break off and go back again and that [pattern] lasted four years. In fact, I went [into analysis] again for about four months this last fall, but I feel I have done about as much as I can in that area and it's time to go ahead and live."

She went into analysis because she thought her abduction caused much of her trouble and she needed to build self-esteem. "I knew that what happened in my childhood was the cause of my problems, but I couldn't deal with it at a very deep level and I wanted to be free of it and go on with my life. I began to realize I had to be responsible for my own life. I've learned to value myself. I didn't think of myself as valuable, because of the way I'd been dumped around and treated."

Doris tried not to let anger tell her what to do. "My father was in a state of anger and passion and worked out this little plan on how to get back at my mother. The only thing I ever heard him say about it, in a half-joking way, was that possession was ninety percent of the law. I could never bring myself to ask my father why he did it."

This experience taught her to make sure her own daughter, now a young teenager, would not suffer from Doris's divorce. "As far as my daughter is concerned, I know that when my own marriage was falling apart, I made an extreme effort to keep an amiable contact with my husband on the issue of how we related to our daughter. I know that I bent over backward not to create an atmosphere that would raise his anger," she said.

"My daughter has a good relationship with her father and I think that is due to some degree to my understanding."

She worried, of course, that her *own* daughter might be taken. "In the beginning of our separation, I was in a state of constant anxiety that she would be snatched. That year the novel *Do With Me What You Will* came out and the young woman in the book was kind of passive, and I identified with that a great deal."

Doris Freeman saw her mother, finally, after seventeen years.

"As I grew up, I didn't know where my mother was. I had no way to know," she said. "As it turned out, she married again. She married a man who came back from overseas after the war. They went to Minnesota, to a small town, and I could never have traced her except that I did remember the name of her brother and I found him in the library. He had a Ph.D. and I traced him through *American Men of Science.*

"I was able to write him when I was twenty-one. My father didn't respond at all. He simply said that I was old enough and it was my own life. I went to Chicago where my uncle was and my mother joined me there and we went back to Minnesota from there for a month and we have written to each other ever since. It was strange. After all, I hadn't seen her since I was four years old.

"She didn't feel she had any way to get me, she said. She didn't feel that she had anyone to back her up. My feeling was that they could have used rational means to handle their differences, because it wasn't so much a custody battle in this case as it was anger at each other.

"My mother was twenty-seven at the time of the abduction and my father was thirty-four. I think the act was so sudden and brutal in the way it occurred that she was traumatized. She was ill and upset and it took her months to overcome the shock, she told me. By that time I was across the country and she simply did not know what to do. Also, she didn't have the money to fly.

"She told me she was convinced there was no way she could get hold of me. And the best thing for her, she thought, was to start a new life. She married again, but wasn't able to have more children. She and her husband led a very quiet, loving life. They adopted two children and she never told anyone of me. In some way, I think she was afraid.

"When I came forward, I learned that her husband had died just six months before, and so when I came it was a very positive thing in her life. Then she was able to tell people in this little town in Minnesota.

"Apparently it did her a great deal of good to get back in touch with me."

16

Parents:
The Emotional Impact

Child stealing takes a toll on parents, too.

First they weep, then they try the system. A brush with the law shows how alone they are. Hurt turns to anger then, cries become screams. Lawyers cannot help. Investigators run into dead ends. Both cost money. Many parents mortgage their homes, borrow from relatives, drain savings, use up credit.

Then they turn bitter, hostile, sour. If they don't find their children in a few months, many become apathetic and give up.

It is hopeless, they feel, to try and change society. State and federal bills, if passed, won't help, they say. Why bother? Losing children makes them selfish. All they want is to get them back. Who cares, they ask, if a law passes next year? What could it do for me *now*?

Parents withdraw in a combination of anger and apathy. They have trouble getting up each morning. Their lives stop —emotions frozen, jobs abandoned, friends and themselves neglected. Houses go uncleaned. They forget to food shop, become absentminded, paralyzed with fear and bitterness. Phones go unanswered, doorbells ignored. Some act like sleepwalkers, eyes glazed, their thinking distracted. Others spend the first day or two after their children are stolen in a burst of energy—calling police, district attorneys, ex-in-laws, friends, driving hundreds of miles through the night to where they last knew their children were—only to find their spouse's house empty.

Some write politicians, asking for help, saying they are going to picket city hall until their children come back. Red tape stops them. One official sends them to another. "It isn't a *city* problem, it's a *state* one," they are told. "*We* can't do anything, *either*," state officials say. "Call the FBI." Bureau agents send them home again. "Start with your local police," they say, "or county authorities."

Parents give up. They were going to write letters, rally friends, neighbors, the public to their cause. But after several days they don't know where to picket. They soon learn that no one understands their problem.

Very quickly, exhaustion—emotional and physical—sets in. Friends of one woman in Long Island had to break into her house a week after she'd lost her children. They found her asleep in an armchair before a late movie on television. She wore the same clothes they'd seen her in a week before. Two empty cartons of cigarettes were on the floor. She'd filled two ashtrays, then begun stamping out her cigarettes on the rug with her bare feet.

The woman, Gail Heinman, admitted she hadn't eaten in four days. Her friends felt she was in shock and took her to the emergency room of a local hospital. She was kept under observation for two weeks. Friends took her home and she lived with them several months, until she could return home and start working part-time.

Heinman found her two children, both girls, ages eight and six, in San Diego a year later. Laws couldn't help because she didn't have custody. Her husband left while they were still married.

This Long Island mother flew to San Diego, hired an investigator recommended by the Los Angeles group, the

Stolen Children Information Exchange, and recovered her children on the way home from school.

Gail Heinman's reaction to child stealing is not unusual. Private investigator George Cerone described similar symptoms. "Any parent who loses a child suffers," he said. "Parents have dropped out of work, become withdrawn, lost weight. The victimized parent shows a definite physical effect.

"I've seen women go from one hundred thirty-five pounds down to ninety-eight pounds in a month. They become introverted, depressed, worried all the time. They come in as a last resort. They've tried the courts, been turned down by law enforcement. There's nobody else left.

"They ask what did they do to deserve this. They blame their husband, of course. They cry out of fear and concern for their children. They've seen their marriage break up and they cry for that, too. Their friends can only offer advice. Courts tell them, 'We can't do anything because we don't know where they are.' "

Another parent whose child was stolen told how he felt up until the time he actually picked up his son in Manhattan.

Robert Bogin, a twenty-nine-year-old dental technician from Buffalo, New York, spent four months looking for his six-year-old son in Manhattan about a year ago. He had temporary custody of the boy, but his ex-wife vanished before there was a hearing on permanent custody.

Then one Saturday afternoon in the fall of 1979 she took their son off a playground in Buffalo. Her family helped. Bogin learned she lived in Manhattan from former neighbors of hers, where she had lived in Queens before disappearing. They gave him a forwarding address and he watched her apartment, seeing her sometimes, but not the boy, during that four-month search.

"Every day I held a little vigil in front of her apartment building," he said, "hoping she would come out. I sat there from morning until night, every day. I wore a hat and false moustache and had a rented car, so she couldn't tell it was me. I took a month's leave from my job."

It was a struggle for him, thinking he knew where his son was, but not seeing him. "I was a wreck," he said. "There were actual physical differences in me after this happened. I was fatigued, worn out, and had stomach pains. I became very lethargic about everything. It was a case of just staying alive, just staying sane and rational. Of being able to drive my car to where I could watch the apartment and not have an accident along the way."

Bogin, too, tried the law. "Finally, after all this watching, I went to two lawyers in New York City," he said. "They contacted the judge in Buffalo who'd been on the case and all I got was closed doors. My lawyers both advised me, off the record, to just get my son. That was the only recourse left."

Their advice made him sick. "I went into a luncheonette in Manhattan and bought soup and toast. I was starved. But my stomach couldn't hold food. I felt so helpless, as if all of society was against me. There was a mad dash to the men's room where I threw up."

He went back to the streets. "It was so frustrating," he said, "sitting in a car from morning until night, day after day. I was as close as I'll ever come to a nervous breakdown. I had no way of contacting my boy. I *had* to find him and deep down knew eventually I would.

"I kept my vigil. Finally, one day it paid off. I got to her apartment about seven o'clock in the morning and around nine A.M. he came out, walking his dog. I went up to him and told him that I was there to take him home. He said, 'Okay.' He was glad to see me, and we got in the car. My sister had come to keep me company and we drove right over to New Jersey and got on a plane to Buffalo," Bogin said.

He feared a second child theft, as do all parents who re-cover their children. It almost happened, too. "My ex-wife came up to my office and the boy was playing outside," he said. "It was a Saturday and my son came running in, screaming, 'My mommy's out there and she wants me to come with her.' He hid under the desk."

Bogin wouldn't let her see their son. "I said, 'That's it. We could have had a good thing for our child and I was willing to bend, but now I can't trust you.' She hasn't tried to see him or talk to him since."

Bogin was so afraid she'd take their boy again he went into hiding. "My ex-wife doesn't know where I am and probably thinks I'm still in Buffalo," he said. He lives on eastern Long Island now, where he works in a hospital. Still fearful, not completely relaxed or secure even though his son is home, he watches the boy closely.

"I don't let him go on the school bus because this is where they sometimes get picked up," he said. "I don't take chances. He's taken to school and picked up there. I'm alert. If I see a strange car on my street or anything that looks suspicious, I'll go down the back stairs of the apartment.

"My car is never parked in front of the same building. It's always in back, in front of the *next* apartment, somewhere. I try never to park it in the same place twice."

One reason for Bogin's fear is that he believes his wife will neglect their son if he is stolen again. The first time, "she didn't care for him the way he was used to being cared for when we had him," he said. "She left him alone a lot, he told me, with baby-sitters, and he was upset about this. She always had people coming over who weren't very pleasant. He is a mild asthmatic and was wheezing when I picked him up.

"After I got him, he woke up crying once and said he was afraid she would come and take him. *His* waking up made *me* wake up, only more than once. It's, like, once a *week*. I go to the window and see if there are strange cars on the street," he said.

Once their children have been recovered parents generally relax. It ends their worry, "unfreezes" them, so to speak. Allows them to resume normal, or near-normal, lives, until their children grow up and are old enough to use the telephone.

Yet fear persists, danger continues. It usually lasts until their children are old enough to resist another attempt to steal them—whether by running away or fighting the abductor(s) off. Most parents of recovered children will immediately teach their children about area codes and zip codes. They will drill their children on *exactly* how to write their home addresses. They will tell them to use the telephone when the parent is asleep or out of the house. All the while, they try not to let children know they are afraid of a second child theft.

But it doesn't always work. A Milwaukee, Wisconsin, mother recovered her seven-year-old daughter from Boston, Massachusetts, after a nine-month search. The mother, Myra Cosinsky, overreacted to the child theft. "I tried not to make my daughter afraid, as *I* was afraid," she said. "But we had a little kidnap drill. I'd sit her down and fire questions at her: What's my name? Where do I live? What's our phone number here?

"The little tot knew we lived in Milwaukee, but we'd moved since she came home so that her father couldn't find her. She had trouble with our new address and finally asked, 'Why do I have to know this, Mommy?' I told her it was because she might get lost."

Cosinsky admits she might have gone too far. "I kept sewing dimes and quarters into the hemlines of her dresses," she said. "She wondered why. I said, 'In case you *do* become lost.' She wanted to know why she just couldn't go up to someone and ask directions. I told her she might not be allowed to. That Daddy could steal her again and she might have to use a pay phone in a new school and call me up."

This admission scared her daughter. She began to cry. She couldn't understand why her own parents would keep her away from her friends. "I tried to make her understand that we both loved her and wanted her," Cosinsky said. "But I lost control and said her father was bad for what he'd done. She then felt unloved by him."

Parents whose children have *not* been recovered often remain bitter and can't pick up their lives. Mothers might move in with their parents. Other parents, both men and women, feel they must relocate to new cities, start fresh careers.

Most parents adjust in some way. Their "frozen" period can last several days or several months. At some time, though, they realize that finding their children cannot be their only concern, even if it is the main one. They must go back to work, must start dating, must face the outside world.

This is easier for women who have jobs outside their homes. They may stay home a few days or weeks, but usually they get back to a normal routine sooner than housewives do.

Most fathers react like working women. They, too, have responsibilities, professions, things to keep them busy while searching for their children. Fathers, however, generally have more money than mothers do. They are usually older, have worked longer, and can afford lawyers and private investigators, while many mothers can't.

Housewives often feel they've lost their professions—as mothers, as wives—and now they need to retrain, to adjust their thinking. It takes them longer to figure out what to do. One day they have a job they like. The next day their job is taken away. Many women who marry after high school never hold a full-time job, depend on someone else to deal with the outside world. First, it is their parents, then their husbands, now they have no one and usually fall back on their parents again. They feel broken and hate to ask relatives for help, especially money for lawyers or investigators. They also feel a certain stigma. Raising children was their only job. Neighbors might think them unfit because their husbands stole the children.

"I couldn't go out on the street for a month," a Seattle woman said. "My friends thought maybe I deserved to lose my baby. There were questions. I didn't hear them directly, of course. But a week after my baby was stolen one of my girlfriends called to say two women down the street thought I must have been a poor wife and mother for my husband to run off like that."

These women can lose friends just when they need them the most. Sometimes there are rumors that they were unfit, neglected their children, didn't keep house neatly. Fathers who steal children before a custody hearing often try to build a case against their wives. They say they *had* to steal the child. Court papers show up with allegations of neglect and abuse, false reports of times when the man of the house came home and found his wife gone, his son or daughter playing with matches near a lighted stove, knives and scissors on the floor, flammable liquids—paints, cleaners— nearby.

"I had to steal them to protect them," some men say. Many husbands will call up friends, neighbors, relatives and spin yarns of infidelity, untidiness, painting portraits of how unfit their wives are.

So in addition to losing their children women may lose their reputations. Now they're tainted. They lose money, support, friends. They may even lose their homes.

Some victimized mothers give up.

They don't forget, of course. Often they keep pictures of their children secret. Some never remarry. Some remarry and don't even tell their new husbands. If they are young enough, they have new children, build new lives. It is hard for them to speak of their former lives, and former children.

They're guilty and defensive. They feel they must make excuses for not looking. They can't afford a search, can't afford court fights, can't afford to raise their children if they recover them. And they don't want to drag child stealing into their new marriages.

Some *do* tell their new husbands. But, still, they don't look.

Marie Ciani, twenty-four, lost her son when she was twenty-one and he was fourteen months. Her ex-husband, a steelworker, left Gary, Indiana, one day in May 1976 with their boy and never returned. Ciani was in college then, studying to be a social worker. She dropped out for a semester, finally returned part-time. Trips to Seattle, Washington, where her ex-husband had relatives, and Des Moines, Iowa, where he had friends, were dead ends. They didn't tell her anything.

"I looked for a year," Ciani said. "My parents were very supportive. They paid for my trips. They paid my tuition. But there came a point, and we all agreed what I should do.

"It was about six months after the baby was gone," she explained. "My mother said to me one night after dinner, 'This isn't your whole life.' She told me of women who'd lost children to sudden infant death syndrome and accidents, respiratory diseases, other illnesses. She said it was time to pick up."

Ciani went back to college full time, earned her degree. She couldn't think of remarrying, at first. But she was still young. "I had to think of the life *ahead* of me, not *behind*," she said. "I wanted it to be full."

She started dating in 1978, an older man who'd been one of her teachers. "He was thirty-two and had just gotten his Ph.D. when I met him," Ciani said. "He was divorced but didn't have any children. I told him from the beginning about my baby and he understood. I said that someday, when I was ready, I'd have to start looking. But a new marriage and family came first. He accepted that and we were engaged."

They married in 1979. Both worked. He got a job with a

two-year college in Illinois, north of Chicago, and she became a county caseworker. They had their first child in 1980, a girl.

"I wondered what would have happened to me if the baby had been a boy," Ciani said. "But having a little girl helped. It wasn't like I was repeating with a son again. I might not have been able to take that. Yet, we were prepared. We'd been to therapy before we left Indiana and agreed not to tell anyone in Illinois about my first baby."

There was guilt, of course, and they talked about it to each other. "He supported me and helped," Ciani said. "Because I've never forgotten my son. A year after he'd been stolen I had ulcers and then George, my new husband, came along and I pulled out of it. Ever since, he seems to know when I'm depressed and takes me out to dinner. It really hit me every few months, and still does."

At one point they considered hiring an investigator. Her new husband was for it. But she declined. It would be too trying, she said, too painful. Their new friends would find out. It could become a curse, occupying them every day as it had Marie that first year.

"It could destroy my second marriage," she said. "I mean, I would have to drop everything. And if we *did* find him, then what? We couldn't move. My son might not remember me. He might be better off where he was."

Marie and George have their own therapy—those dinners out, their long talks, their new baby. "Looking for my son would remind me of my first marriage, which was a mistake from the beginning," Marie said. "It would open too many closed doors."

Other parents can't adjust like Marie Ciani, though. They can't let go, might not want to settle down. They feel that if they *do* find their stolen children they might want to move and be near them. They can't start new families because they worry over their lost children. Who should receive more attention? New children? Stolen children? What if they remarried, had babies, *then* found their sons or daughters? Where should they live? It wouldn't be fair to new children to suddenly run off to visit or recover those first children. It might not be fair to new spouses, either.

"I'm working now and feel I have a career ahead of me," said Jennifer Swanson, twenty-seven, who works in the personnel division of a large department store in Philadelphia, Pennsylvania. "But I can fly out on a day's notice. And since I'm single, I could live on little money until I found a new job. People here understand and would recommend me."

Jennifer isn't looking. There are a lot of excuses. "How can I look? I work nine to five. My lawyer says an investigator would want five thousand dollars and he, the attorney, wants a two-thousand-dollar retainer in case I need more legal work."

She has custody of her daughter, who was four years old when she was stolen in 1977. "My apartment is too small. My ex-husband would kill me if I found him. My child has a stable life. A psychologist told me I'd disrupt that life, perhaps ruin it, if I popped in now. She told me my daughter probably has a stepmother now and would be confused. Suddenly she'd have two mothers."

Jennifer has had several relationships with men, but has broken them off, feeling her lovers didn't understand. "They told me I had a cross to bear," she said. "And maybe I do. But they couldn't understand my depression sometimes."

She said they told her she should find her daughter, break the tension and questioning, that even if her daughter rejected her, the wondering would be over.

"But I couldn't do that," Jennifer said. "It's *much* too painful. I know I'm limping along. But I know there's a man out there who *will* understand and accept me."

A psychologist told her she asked too much. New husbands would want a fresh start, not a woman with a past she couldn't live down. "It was that past which she [the psychologist] thought I should forget. Yet, I can't," Jennifer said.

An attractive redhead with smooth skin and green eyes, Jennifer has an active social life. But she can't form lasting, meaningful relationships, and knows it. Every day she goes to work she carries a picture of her daughter with her. Once, on her daughter's birthday, she took too many sleeping pills. Hospital technicians in an emergency room pumped her stomach. She stayed home a week from work.

Holidays are difficult. Friends make sure to include her at parties and dinners. But they let her go off by herself if she wants.

"Maybe what I'm doing *is* wrong," Swanson said. "I know I'm caught. But it could be worse if I began looking for her again. After a year of detectives and calling my lawyer I felt it wasn't worth it. I'd come home and look in the mail, make phone calls, stay up late reading maps and wonder which state she might be in. I'd lost weight and decided I just couldn't live that way. Half a life—the kind I have now—is better than none."

Jennifer Swanson is now engaged. She and her fiancé have gone for counseling to ease her burden and to bring him into her problem. She thinks it's working.

Some parents who do remarry don't tell their new husbands or wives. They tell their new children they love them, and keep pictures of their stolen children hidden. One Ohio mother went into the attic once and found her six-year-old daughter by her new husband playing with a friend near an old trunk.

"It had pictures from my first wedding," the mother, Constance Negrilli, thirty-one, said. "And baby pictures of my stolen son. Thank God the girls didn't open it."

She sent them downstairs and sat by herself, shaking. "It was the closest I've come to breaking down," she said. "I'd kept the child stealing a secret, hadn't told anyone, even my new husband.

Negrilli had gone through the usual withdrawal stage after her child had been stolen nine years before. But she wanted a new family and didn't work outside the home. Her new marriage was all she had and she didn't want it to break.

"I'd put the child stealing out of my mind, first with therapy and then with self-control. But I just couldn't throw away those pictures. Maybe someday I'll tell my family, when my present child is older," she said.

Her second husband is a bank vice-president. She feels telling her story would hurt his reputation, make her seem a fallen woman, scarred, unfit, damaged. That self-control has held during her stolen child's birthdays and over holidays. She gets through them by keeping busy.

"Every year on my first child's birthday I bake a cake," Negrilli said. "I tell people it's for an aunt who died years ago, a woman I knew as a child and loved. They accept that. At Christmas I have big dinners, work and cook all day. Afterward, if I'm depressed, I tell people I'm just tired. They think I'm a good hostess and everyone at the bank looks forward to my parties on Christmas Eve."

She and her second husband have reputations as community leaders. Negrilli doesn't know what she'd do if her stolen child appeared someday. "I know I'd take him in," she said. "And I know I'd have to tell people. But it's a decision I keep putting off. Yet there's always the chance. Maybe someday I'll bare my heart. But what good would it do now? I have a rewarding life. There's too much at stake."

Then there are parents who find their children, but can't recover them. Some have no money to fund a court fight in new states. Mothers may be afraid their ex-husbands will beat them. They don't want a hassle. It might be easier to live with a new situation, to give up custody in return for a quiet life.

It is better to know where children are, parents feel, and see them on weekends or holidays, than to chase them around the country. It is better to speak with an ex-spouse and visit with a child than to fight—in court, over the phone, on the street, wherever, whenever.

It might also save a parent's life.

One New York City mother spent twenty thousand dollars on lawyers and expenses, won custody of her son in two courts, but only visits with him now. The boy, who is four, was stolen in November 1978, on a weekend when his father came to visit. His mother, Beth Cole, thirty-one, is a health and physical education professor at a university in the New York metropolitan area. Her ex-husband, Michael, thirty-six, is a building contractor.

Beth Cole had no idea where her little boy was until July 1979, when Michael called from Atlantic City, New Jersey. "I think that deep down he knew what he was doing was wrong," she said. "He wanted our son because he feels he can't live if he can't talk with him every day."

Though she won custody, Beth only spends weekends with her son. Of her ex-husband she says, "We had one fight, and I ended up in the emergency room of an Atlantic City hospital with a couple of stitches in my lip when I got out of line with him."

She felt helpless, the victim of a violent husband and indifferent courts. She did everything right—hired lawyers, paid them herself, won custody, stayed in the system—and lost. Her husband beat her, stole their son; New Jersey ignored New York's custody order.

Of the brutality, she said: "I decided not to press charges. It would only have cost him a hundred-dollar fine—it was a misdemeanor—and it might have aggravated him more. He could hit me again or not let me see Stan. I chose to see my son."

She often rides to Atlantic City from Manhattan to pick up her son and bring him "home" to her apartment for weekends. It is strained. "Even though I'm seeing him," she said, "I'm still a captive to what my ex-husband says. Since he stole my car, I take the bus. I've been bringing Stan back here since the last hassle in Atlantic City. On Friday I go down. It's a two-and-a-half-hour bus ride. I pick him up and get back here about five o'clock in the afternoon. We have Friday night and Saturday to visit and a little bit on Sunday morning and then I take him back."

Beth thought of snatching her son and hiding. But she was afraid her ex-husband would find her and kill her, he felt so strongly about his son.

"The point that everyone makes is that I simply should not return Stan," she said. "But I'm not ready to disappear. I don't want to do that. I'd have to go to another country and assume a totally different name and fake identity. I'm too established in this country right now. Also, would that be good for Stan? I'd have to do something like be a waitress or a secretary and I wouldn't be happy and couldn't earn a good living.

"I could be found in this country. I'm convinced my ex-husband would come and take him again. He walked out of three businesses and established himself again.

"The solution, is to be happy with what I have. In a few years, Stan might say, 'Hey, I want to live with my mother.' I'm waiting for that. It could be long, though, because my husband will never give up unless he gets involved with another woman who hates Stan and wants a child of her own, but I know how long off that is. I'm living with it."

Beth Cole, a mother in exile, teaching during the week, riding buses on Fridays into a hostile state to "recover" her stolen child and bring him to Manhattan for "lost weekends," felt she and her son were doing the best they could.

17

Reunions

Many parents must wait as long as ten years or more before finding their children.

They might lose them as babies, and not find them until they are teenagers. Many give up after a year or two. It's a part of them they want to forget. Some remarry, start new families; others stay single, afraid to try again. Almost all of them fear that, once found, their children will reject them. Both parent and child have new lives now. What would they do with a strange teenager? A new parent? How could it work out?

It works out the same as finding lost relatives. Only it's more tense, painful. There is usually a short, nervous reunion. Maybe they will have a short visit, or dinner, or a talk. It isn't long. By this time they have such different routines—parents with jobs and family at home in another state; children with school, friends, activities in the new state. Most parents don't want to startle their "found" children, who fear being taken away from what they know *now* as their lives.

A reunion can be tearful, joyous, heartbreaking, happy. It can also be frightening. A parent is seeing a child who is grown, a stranger who's been raised by someone else. And a child suddenly has a new parent, someone besides the father or mother who stole him or her years ago, or an uncle or aunt who has raised him or her. They don't know each other. Meeting a distant cousin, a long-lost relative, is a happy celebration. Meeting your long-lost parent or stolen child often is not. It hurts to open old wounds.

Catherine Denise, forty-two, is a waitress in Freeport, New York, on Long Island's south shore. She and her former husband, James, a union official, had lived in Toronto, Canada, with their two girls, who were six and seven years old. This was in 1967, the year they divorced. She won custody.

But Catherine Denise was ill. She went to stay with her parents in England and came back to Canada to find her ex-husband and children gone. She also learned he'd had the custody order overturned: Now the children were his.

She moved to Long Island because her ex-husband had family there. She was hoping she could learn where her daughters were by living near their paternal grandparents.

"As it happened," she said, "James lived on Long Island, too, but the children were in boarding school in Albany. I served papers on him, asking that he produce the children in court. I also wanted a new hearing on custody. I hadn't been notified of the second one in Canada."

James Denise disappeared again. He took their children out of school. In July 1968, he wrote Catherine from Minneapolis and told how they could arrange a visit. He'd remarried and had put their children in a Vermont school. He gave her a psychiatrist's name there who would set up the visit.

"The psychiatrist told me to come for an examination," she said. "He wanted to learn my background and determine if I was fit to see my daughters.

"I said it was none of his business, but if he brought the children to his office, I would come up."

She went to Vermont and saw him. But he said she'd have to come back again and wouldn't give her the name of their school. "I don't even know if they *were* in school there," she said. "I didn't go up again."

Catherine Denise returned to England, confused, scared. She was in a hospital for a while with exhaustion. What could she do? She had no money, couldn't hire investigators. She had a copy of the second Toronto court order; it gave her visitation on weekends and in the summer. But weekends and summers *where*?

She returned to Freeport and got a job as a waitress, close to her former father-in-law. He still wouldn't say anything. Would he tell his son to stay away? She wanted to watch his home on holidays. But it was too much. Moving seemed her only choice, an escape.

There were other jobs, other towns, other trips to England. Catherine Denise couldn't marry again. She felt part of her was still married, a part which included two girls. She was a mother. She had a family, of sorts, an incomplete life. It was hard to begin a new one, she felt, until she cleared up her *old* one, until she found her children.

So she moved to Freeport again, hoping that her former father-in-law had forgotten her and would become careless and let his grandchildren visit.

She had hired a private investigator once, but he hadn't found anything. She didn't want to hire another one. So she waited, prayed her ex-husband would bring the children to his father's house. Long Island's south shore is a nice place to summer, she thought. James might send the girls there. He couldn't have them in boarding school during July and August. Camp might be too expensive. His father had a nice home, a few blocks from the water, and a boat.

She was right. On Memorial Day weekend 1978, eleven years after she'd last seen them, she ran into one of her daughters on the beach.

"I lived in an apartment near the docks where I could keep an eye on his house," she said. "I knew what beach my former father-in-law used, where he docked his boat. I was down by the water that weekend and saw one of my daughters walk by with her grandparents. I knew what they [the grandparents] looked like, of course, and figured the girl with them must be one of my daughters.

'It was on the dock that I saw her. I approached them and said to the girl, 'Is your name Jane or Cecilia?' She smiled and told me, 'Yes.'

"Although I hadn't intended to shock her, I said, 'I'm your mother.'

"But I was a stranger to her and it surprised her to have me suddenly be there. She wasn't prepared for it. She backed off and headed for the boat, a couple of yards away. I said, 'Tell your sister I've been looking for you, but your father keeps taking you away.'

"I could see she was in a state of shock and was very frightened, so I didn't pursue it. I walked down by the dock a half hour later. They all sat on his boat. I wanted to give her time to relax, to think, and didn't approach her again. It was scary.

"Later, when her grandfather was alone, I said I was going to take him to court. I had a lawyer write him, but he never wrote back."

She called her former father-in-law, then. He told her the children had gone and wouldn't return. "I finally decided to try real hard to find my ex-husband," she said. Through an investigator she got his phone bill.

The investigator came up with a phone number and a street address in Minneapolis. But she was afraid to call. She didn't want to startle her daughters again. And she didn't want her ex-husband to know she'd found him. He might run again. She had the investigator check schools in the Minneapolis–St. Paul area. In the fall of 1978, she learned her oldest daughter was in a two-year college there.

It took Catherine Denise three months to gain the courage to write. She called one of the college's counselors and they both decided a letter would be best. "I didn't want to go marching in there and surprise her," Denise said.

"I didn't impulsively get on a plane and go out there, either, when I learned about the college. After not having seen her in so many years, everything was suppressed, I suppose. You want to see your children, but don't *dare* be impulsive, not where they are concerned. They are young women now and very independent."

Her daughter wrote back, and gave her the address where the second daughter was, another private boarding school. Catherine Denise wrote there, too, and also received a letter back.

"They were very happy to hear from me," she said. "I sent them all the documents. They were never told anything derogatory about me. They were told nothing. Just that everything was for their own good, their father had said. That's all they ever knew. Of course, they are older now and went through all the documents and saw what actually had happened.

"I sent them copies of everything, court orders which showed I had custody originally and then visitation. It brought back their past, how they'd been moved so much.

"But what they needed was time," she said. "*I* needed time, too. I wrote and they would answer and sometimes when I wouldn't hear from them I thought their father had stopped them," she said.

It was almost a year before Catherine Denise saw her daughters in Minnesota.

"They invited me for Christmas in 1979 and everything turned out great," she said. "I'm so glad I didn't just go out there without writing. When you meet your children after a long period you can't be abrupt. You have to give them time to realize who you are and that you're not going to yank them away again, that their lives aren't going to change drastically."

She described their first meeting. It was in the older girl's apartment. There was small talk for the first few hours. How was the flight? How was Long Island's winter compared to Minnesota's?

"I apologized to my one daughter for scaring her that day on the beach and told her how desperate I'd been," she said.

"I said there was no other way I could have reached her. She understood. Her grandfather only told her I must have been mistaken and that she should forget the incident.

"Evidently my daughter *didn't* forget and wrote a long letter to her father that night. But she tore it up."

Of their reunion in Minnesota, Denise said: "I dressed up, but they were casual. I felt I should have been more casual, too. There was no big emotional scene. It was just like I hadn't seen them for a few months. As the days went by and we talked, we grew closer. I stayed two weeks."

They told their mother what their lives had been like.

"They hadn't been happy," she said. "They'd been very lonely at times. They were always switching schools and living in foster homes. One of them ran away once. It was hard to listen to them and know that I hadn't been there to help."

They'd moved from Canada to the States and had been separated for a while. One was in school in New Jersey and the other in Maryland. First, it was foster homes; when they were older, boarding schools.

"He was always sending them away," she said. "His second wife didn't want them around."

Yet seeing their mother brought the girls closer. All three are like old friends now. "They're very open with me and I think that's good. One daughter said that within those two weeks, she felt she'd known me all her life."

But Catherine Denise realized her daughters were grown. "It's a bit late for me to step in and start playing Mommy," she said.

She spoke of how she got through those long years without them. "At times I nearly gave up," she said. "It becomes more frightening as time passes. You get over the emotional shock of losing them and have to get yourself together. Not totally, but as much as you can. You have to pick up the pieces, begin living again."

Catherine Denise felt that finding her children was right,

both for herself and for them. It ended a mystery, broke tension, started new, better lives for each of them.

"It did wonders for my children," she said. "Particularly with their father remarrying and their feeling not wanted. They may grow to hate him for it, but I tried not to encourage that. The past is over."

They thanked her for how she came to see them. "In the first letter my daughter wrote, she said, 'Mom, I want to thank you very much for the way you did this. You've left us freedom of choice, which is something we've rarely had.'"

June Gratin found her daughter after twelve years of separation. But the reunion was difficult and delicate, one that is still being worked out. She lost her daughter, Donna, in August 1968, when the child was two. She and her husband had divorced in 1968, and she went to live with her parents in Patchogue, New York; he rented an apartment in a town nearby. Her husband, Preston, was twenty-five years old then, an airline reservations clerk, and June was twenty-three.

"We started having trouble after the baby was born," June Gratin said. "Donna was only two months old and something went wrong and he was in a terrible rage. I locked myself in one room of our house and he banged on the door and threatened to kill me. He had psychological problems. The judge gave him only one hour a week to see Donna when we had our hearing. The baby was almost two then," she said.

On August 15, 1968, June Gratin called Preston to see if he wanted to visit with Donna. They agreed to meet in an arboretum. "We walked around for a while that afternoon," she said, "and then went into a greenhouse they had there. I asked him to hold Donna while I went to freshen up.

"When I came out, they were gone," she said.

Just like that.

Gone.

After five years of searching, June, with the help of her

sister, Johanna, had tracked her daughter to the home of
Preston's sister and brother-in-law in North Miami, Florida.
But June, now remarried and pregnant, was ordered by her
doctor to stop the search. It was too great a strain on her.
Her sister, Johanna, though, didn't give up. A mother of two
elementary school children herself, she kept after her sister.
But Johanna waited until 1980 to make her move. In April,
she went to North Miami, to the home of Preston's sister and
brother-in-law, Gerard and Paula. Johanna figured that
Donna, who was thirteen in January 1980, would be in
school during the day. She learned from a neighbor when
classes were over in the afternoon. Then she parked half a
block away. She was alone.

Three girls walked by the car. They stopped in front of
Gerard and Paula's home. One of them went up the driveway. Johanna knew she must be her sister's stolen daughter.

"I went to her and was a little out of breath," Johanna
said. "I didn't want to scare her, but didn't want her going
into the house, either. I said, 'Is your name Donna?'

"The girl looked at me. 'Yes,' she said. 'Who are you?' A
friend of your father's from New York,' I told her.

"Donna was curious. What was I doing there? Where did
I live? What did I want? I just told her I was visiting in
Miami and had driven by, a chance meeting. Then I left,"
Johanna said.

She flew home. June Gratin, who by now had two new
children by her second husband—both girls, seven and three
—was scared. Johanna said they should go to Florida right
away. The more June thought about it, the weaker she felt.

They left for Florida a week later, and went to the school
where Donna was enrolled. They got there in the morning,
as buses emptied, and went to the principal's office. June
Gratin told him what she wanted. He called Donna in.

But the girl saw Johanna and ran out of school, frightened. Gerard and Paula lived only a few blocks away. June
and Johanna followed her.

"We got to the house as she ran into it," June said. "Her uncle, Gerard, stood outside. Of course, there have been very bad feelings between him and me for years. He was the controlling factor. He threatened to call the police and I told him to go ahead, but that this was not the time for police and courts. I wasn't moving and was going to see my daughter.

"He looked drawn and tired," June said, "like he'd been caught. I told him I wasn't there to tear her away from anything and he said there was no way he would let me take her out of Florida. I asked where my ex-husband was and he told me that if I wanted to know, I'd have to find him myself.

"I said, 'I haven't been able to find him for eleven years. How do you expect me to find him now?' He told me, 'That's *your* problem.' Then he went to call his wife, Paula, and have *her* tell Donna what was going on before I could see her," June said.

They waited forty minutes in Gerard's driveway, until Paula came home from work. There were a few more minutes of waiting. June almost lost her nerve. Johanna wouldn't let her. They sat in the car and finally Paula came out and said it was all right and June went in by herself. Gerard, Paula, and Johanna stayed on the lawn.

"Donna wore blue jeans and a red shirt and sat on her bed," June said. "She told me that she hadn't seen her father in six years and that he'd told me I was dead."

June's daughter was afraid. She didn't want to leave North Miami, didn't know whom to believe.

"Even so, our first meeting was very good," June said. "She was warm and accepting and just terrific. I showed her pictures and gave her an old doll that belonged to her."

They talked about what had happened. Donna's father had taken her to California after leaving the arboretum that day. He traveled by himself with her and kept in touch with Gerard. Preston moved for five years—to Texas, Pennsylvania, even New York for a while, in addition to California. Like so many child stealers, he stayed with relatives and was always ahead of June. He went to Florida when Gerard and Paula moved there.

Preston lost his job as a salesman in Miami and asked his brother and sister-in-law to watch Donna on weekends. He began to leave her with them for long periods. Weekends stretched into weeks. He became a noncustodial parent and would visit his stolen child for a day or two on Saturday or Sunday, even though he lived nearby.

Then Preston didn't come to see his daughter anymore.

"Donna told me she would sit by the window weekend after weekend, waiting for him to come back," June said. "But he never did. It was hard for her to talk. Here people had been lying to her all her life. Her father, her uncle, her aunt, people she trusted. I didn't want to question her, fill her with hate. The girl just looked at me and I gave her a handkerchief and we hugged and I couldn't see because there was so much water in my eyes, too.

"She was crying and saying she was afraid she would never see her mother and that she always wanted a brother or sister and wondered if she had one. She didn't want to believe her father and used to pray at night that he was wrong, that her mother *wasn't* dead. She said she always wanted a *real* home, to belong somewhere," June said.

They spent only an hour together. June Gratin didn't want to overdo their reunion. Donna needed time to think. She had her life and didn't want to give it up, at least not yet. June and Johanna stayed for two weeks, in a motel, gave Donna their number, and kept in touch by phone. One night Donna was playing softball. Her mother and aunt came to watch.

"They were late for the game and I was nervous," June said. "When they came, Donna avoided me. Her uncle came up and said she was afraid I was going to take her away. They'd told her I wouldn't do that. We arranged to take

Donna to dinner one night, just myself and Johanna. He said it was all right."

June Gratin fought to be civil. She had to ask to see her own child—ask people who'd raised her for seven years and who had never called her, not even after Preston had left.

"At dinner in a restaurant, I told Donna that I wanted her to learn to love me, as I've always loved her," June said. "But it had to come naturally. I didn't feel she should force it, I told her. I wouldn't do her any favors by taking her from the only home and security she's known for years. She's close to two cousins and is holding her own in school, after having problems in the first and second grades. Her father traveled so much she missed a lot of school."

Their dinner was tense. Donna said it was hard to believe she had two sisters. June wanted her to come north for a visit, but it was too soon. Donna said she wanted her mother to go home for now.

"Then I mentioned that her uncle had spoken to her father and told him I was here," June said. "Donna asked, 'Did *he* call first, or did my *uncle* call first? I wish I had spoken to him.' On the way home I asked if she wanted to go shopping with me the following day, and she said she didn't know but would call in the morning.

"When I left her, I was very upset. They'd lied to her about her father again, hadn't told her they'd spoken with him since I'd come down. Paula called me at the motel and was angry. I said, 'As far as her father is concerned, Donna has a right to know that you are in touch with him. She has questions which need to be answered and I certainly think she needs to talk with someone other than you and me.'

"Paula promised to speak with the school principal and ask his advice," June said.

June Gratin kept in control. Another family had raised her daughter—without telling her, without her permission. Here she was in a rented room asking to speak to and see her own child. It made her angry, depressed, frustrated, all at once.

Nearly twelve years of searching had come to a strained couple of weeks in a motel in a strange city, with hostile ex-in-laws telling her what she could and couldn't do with her Donna.

"She would have been a different girl if I had raised her," June said. "She's passive, keeps to herself. I could have given her so much, but feel in order to keep her, I have to let her go, give her a chance to choose."

It was a relief to June to find her, though, to know Donna was all right. There was fear in not knowing where she was, what she did, what she was like, not seeing report cards from school, health records from doctors. She tried to hide her resentment toward Gerard and Paula.

"I was talking to Paula before we left and she said that at times she was sorry she didn't know me," June said. "There were times when her heart went out to me, she said, but she didn't know what to do.

"Those words coming from Paula now didn't do anything for me. I said, 'Maybe it would have been easier if you'd called me after her father had left.' She just told me she didn't know what to do."

The whole experience is one that will take June and Donna a long time to get over. "Donna holds things in," June Gratin said. "She's very quiet, doesn't make friends easily, faints in crowds even. She's insecure and needs time and understanding." For June, "There was no end to it, to the search. It was like burying my child, yet knowing she wasn't dead. I was horrified. In a way, it was worse than death. Because there was the not knowing. I realize what families go through with sons and fathers missing in war. You keep wondering, hoping, and that keeps you awake."

June's second husband, who teaches science at a junior high school, told her she'd better not stay home because she needed to get out and keep busy. So she went to college, one course a semester, then full time. She earned a degree to teach elementary school, and sometimes is a substitute teacher besides being a full-time mother and house-wife.

"I decided there were only two ways to go, down or up, and I was going too far down and thought that if I ever found Donna and wanted to be any kind of a mother to her, and to my new children, too, I'd better keep myself going," she said.

June and Donna are slowly building up the relationship that was for so long denied them. On Mother's Day 1980, about a month after she'd found her daughter, June got a call. It was at four o'clock in the afternoon.

There was a weak voice on the other end, static on the line.

"Hello? Is June there?"

"Yes, this is she."

"Hi, Mom. It's Donna."

18

The Parental Kidnapping Prevention Act—Pro

Since 1973 there have been several bills introduced in Congress to stop child stealing. None have passed.

In 1973 Congressman Charles Bennett of Florida, sponsored a bill in the House of Representatives to remove parental exemption from the federal kidnapping statute. The House Judiciary Committee's subcommittee on crime held hearings on it during 1974, but did nothing.

Bennett introduced his bill again, altering it so that it required only a $1,000 fine or a year in prison, or both, for child stealing. Such proposed penalties are much less severe than those for kidnapping. The subcommittee on crime again took no action on the proposed law.

The bill went nowhere, either in 1976 or 1977.

In the Senate, Malcolm Wallop sponsored a similar bill. It passed the Senate in 1978 and again in 1980. But, like the House bill, it died when it went before the House subcommittee.

In 1979, Congressman Bennett and Senator Wallop worked together and introduced similar bills into both houses of Congress. More than twenty senators cosponsored the Wallop bill, S.105; about fifty-five representatives cosponsored the Bennett bill, H.R. 1290.

Senator Edward Kennedy of Massachusetts, Senator George McGovern of South Dakota, Senator Daniel Moynihan of New York, Senators Alan Cranston and S. I. Hayakawa of California, and Senator Strom Thurmond of South Carolina were among the cosponsors of the Senate bill.

There were three main parts of the bills. First, states would have to enforce sister states' custody and visitation orders. In legal terms, this means all states must adopt the Uniform Child Custody Jurisdiction Act, and full faith and credit would be given child custody determinations.

Second, the Federal Parent Locator Service in the United States Department of Health and Human Services would search for parents who violate custody or visitation orders.

Third, it would be a crime to conceal a child for more than seven days in violation of a parent's right of custody or visitation, or to restrain a child without good cause for more than thirty days.

The former offense (a Class B misdemeanor) carries with it a punishment of up to six months in jail, a $10,000 fine, or both. The latter offense (a Class C misdemeanor) carries with it a punishment of up to thirty days, a $10,000 fine, or both.

Both bills said the FBI may look for stolen children. But it cannot start investigating until sixty days after local law enforcement authorities have filed a report and state Parent Locator services, which work with the federal one, ask for help.

Finally, these bills said an alleged abductor will not be charged with child stealing if he or she returns the child or children *unharmed* within thirty days after an arrest warrant has been issued, or if the victimized parents do not report a child snatching within ninety days after it happened.

Criminal sections of these bills, if passed, would have

created a new section of the United States Code called "Parental Kidnapping."

Public hearings on the Senate bill (called the Parental Kidnapping Prevention Act of 1979) were held in January 1980, and on the House bill in May 1980. Speaking at the hearings were senators, lawyers, psychiatrists, representatives of various government agencies—all expressing a wide range of views on the proposed law.

Senator Charles Mathias, who chaired the hearings, summarized the issues: "Snatching parents often take great pains to cover their paths, and substantial cost may be involved in tracking the abductor from state to state. As a result, all too often the parent from whom the child is taken is unable to locate the child and ex-spouse, and the original decree becomes worthless.

"The emotional and economic costs which the parent or legal custodian incurs under present law as the result of a snatching may be very great. In some instances, a distraught parent, finding efforts to regain custody of the child stymied by local law enforcement and the courts, may, in desperation, decide to go it alone and resnatch the child.

"Many parents have plunged into debt, hiring private detectives to search the country for the child, and, once the child is located, traveling to the other state to relitigate the issue of custody.

"But children are the real losers in this desperate game," Mathias said. "Their best interests should be our foremost consideration in any legislative response to the child-snatching problem."

Congressman Bennett discussed another important issue: "It is ridiculous and improper for a parent to have to wage a separate custody battle in state after state because the other parent steals the children and moves to another state. It is tragic when the victimized parent cannot locate the abducted children and may never see them again.

"The emotional strain has been compounded by the problem of finances. It's costly to locate missing children. Private investigators do not come cheap. And once the children are located, the parent may have to travel to that locale and fight for custody in that state's courts.

"And yet, it isn't parents who suffer most. It's children. Most psychiatrists will tell you that after an emotional upheaval, such as divorce, a child must have a stable and secure environment if he or she is to mature properly. The victim of a child snatching is often yanked from a stable environment and thrust into a whole new situation at a very delicate time of his or her development.

"Such a traumatic experience can cause irreparable damage to a child's emotional stability," Bennett said.

Bennett pointed out that most parents steal children before a custody order has been granted. He said S.105 and H.R.1290 would make such stealing a federal crime when there has been *no* state custody order if the restraint or concealment of a child violates a valid written agreement between parents or guardians, or simply violates the natural custodial rights of parents or guardians.

Senator Malcolm Wallop spoke about how child stealing hurts children and how difficult it is for parents to recover children from other states and other countries.

"The psychic, and sometimes physical, harm to the children involved, and to their parents, cannot be underestimated," Wallop said. "A child psychologist from Texas told members of the American Bar Association's Family Law Division that child snatchings induce fear, guilt, and anger in children and have long-lasting, emotionally damaging consequences for the child-victim. Hundreds of parents have written to me describing the terrible ordeal they have experienced," he said.

He also explained that the Supreme Court doesn't require states to recognize each other's custody orders. "The Supreme Court has not interpreted the full faith and credit clause of the Constitution to require states to give full faith and credit recognition to custody decrees entered by a court of another state in an action involving the same parties," he said.

Not only are parents exempt from federal prosecution, he said, but people who steal children for profit can't be arrested on a federal charge, either.

"The detective who is paid handsomely to engineer the abduction may escape criminal liability even where force or the threat of force is involved," Wallop told the hearing.

"We at the federal level have a compelling responsibility to assist states in resolving complicated interstate and international cases," he said. "There is a pressing need to provide some assistance to parents in locating their children and in facilitating the return of the child and abductor-parent to the appropriate state so that decisions affecting access to the child can be made.

"The welfare and well-being of innumerable children is at stake. We have a duty to protect them from the traumatizing experience of being snatched and to see to it that they are restored as quickly as possible to a secure and stable home environment. If we in Congress can establish a strong national policy against child snatching and for a fair adjudication of custody and visitation rights where both fathers and mothers are treated equally, we will have performed an important leadership role. The ultimate winner will be children, parents, and society at large," he said.

Senator Dave Durenberger of Minnesota spoke of how parents in his state had asked his help in finding and recovering their children. He told of meeting parents who have neither seen nor heard from their children for several years —parents who don't know where their children are, or if they are alive or dead—and of meeting children who have suffered the ordeal of kidnapping.

"I've met a little girl who was kidnapped and then recovered. But she bears the scars of that experience, and is spending her childhood in a home for emotionally disturbed children," Durenberger said.

"I've met families that have abandoned their careers and exhausted their financial resources in a futile effort to relocate a kidnapped child.

"And I've spoke with countless families who are not yet victims, but who live every moment with the fear that society's judgment on the custody of their child may be muted by an act of forcible abduction," he said.

The senator explained that parents of stolen children must rely on private attorneys and private detectives. How much money these parents have will determine if they find their children.

"The parents I've met over the past twelve months have invested sums ranging from a minimum of nine thousand dollars to a maximum of forty thousand dollars, in the frequently unsuccessful effort to recover their kidnapped children," Durenberger said. "This is a terrible price, even for those who can raise the money. For those who cannot, the rights conferred by decrees of custody are illusory."

Senator Wallop felt there could be small improvements in his bill. It should be stronger on visitation; the FBI should start on cases without waiting sixty days; and the United States should treat child snatching outside of its limits as a felony.

Also, children should be placed in temporary shelters while awaiting transportation home; the Federal Parent Locator Service should help foreign countries look for children here; and the FBI should study how many child thefts there are in America.

Congressman Robert Duncan of Oregon supported S.105, as did Senators Mathias and Durenberger. But Duncan raised questions about the federal government interfering with state and local domestic disputes.

"How far should government go into social policy?" he

asked. "Should government intervene in a private marital problem? When does it become a public problem?"

He wondered if the federal government should punish a parent for simply moving his or her own child, without harm, across a state. "Are we truly protecting the best interests of the child by tearing him or her away from a parent with whom he or she may have lived for several years, simply because that parent violated a state court decree?" he asked.

Duncan believes that local governments should handle social problems, and would like to have child stealing handled at the state level. Yet he felt that could be difficult. "To do so would require all fifty states to subscribe to the interstate compact [uniform custody laws], both in letter and spirit, and make it impossible for any parent to find a safe haven to harbor a child taken contrary to a court order across a state line," he said.

The congressman felt the federal government has to control child stealing because the state-by-state approach doesn't work. "With this bill we have a means by which to maintain the dynamic federal equilibrium without severe intrusion or imbalance at any level," he said.

19

The Parental
Kidnapping Prevention
Act—Con

The main opposition to the proposed law came from the governmental agencies upon whom the burden of enforcement would fall. Officials from the Department of Justice, FBI, and Department of Health and Human Resources explained at both the Senate and House hearings that they opposed S.105 because the federal government doesn't want to become involved in domestic relations disputes; because FBI agents are overworked already, investigating more serious crimes; and because the Federal Parent Locator Service (FPLS), too, is overworked as well as underfinanced.

Also, they consider use of the FPLS to look for stolen children an invasion of privacy. The service has found absent fathers who ran from support obligations because it has only that *one* purpose, an official said.

"It has long been the department's position that . . . federal law enforcement authorities not become involved in domestic relations disputes," said Paul Michel, acting deputy attorney general of the United States.

There have been exceptions, he explained, where there was clear and convincing evidence that the child was in serious danger of bodily harm as a result of the mental condition or acute behavioral patterns of the abducting parent.

United States attorneys in different parts of the country may review child stealing cases to see if there is that danger, he explained, if there is proof an abducting parent has left his or her home state and, also, if there is a state felony warrant for that person. But only about thirty states consider child stealing a felony, and even among them, a district attorney has powers to choose between either a felony or a misdemeanor warrant.

At the hearing, Michel talked mostly about that part of the bill that would make the federal government find children. Right now, the Parent Locator Service uses Social Security and Internal Revenue Service records to find fathers who run out on support payments. They also use post office records, state tax and employment files, state departments of motor vehicles, and both federal and state corrections agencies to track down these parents.

S.105 would expand the role of the FPLS to let states, courts, and police use those records to find abducting parents. Michel urged the subcommittees to give the civil parts of the bill—in which a state must enforce a custody order made in another state—a chance to work before passing other parts of the bill, those which involve the Parent Locator, the FBI, and would make child stealing a federal crime.

Michel said he didn't like the fact that an abducting parent wouldn't be charged with child stealing if he or she returned the child or children before thirty days had passed since a warrant was issued.

"This provision requires agents to have the wisdom of Solomon," he said. "Suppose an agent, armed with a valid arrest warrant, locates the abducting parent while he or she is returning the child?"

He wondered what the agent should do.

"What if the parent then changes his mind and flees again? One can imagine how difficult it would be for a

United States attorney to prosecute successfully a parent who returns the child on the thirty-first day, but decline to prosecute the parent who returns the child on the twenty-ninth day.

"Secondly, the bill provides that it is an offense to conceal or restrain the child 'without good cause.' That requirement can be expected to present a very real dilemma for a United States attorney's office and the FBI.

"Suppose a parent reports that a child was snatched because of a disagreement between the two separated parents over proper medical treatment or education or religious upbringing of the child.

"Is the FBI supposed to become involved in weighing conflicting points of view or opinions in these areas?

"Also, the abducting parent will likely claim he or she snatched a child because behavior patterns, life-style, or living arrangements of the custodial parent were hurting that child."

Michel told the hearing he felt it would be hard to define *restraint* and *conceal*. An abducting parent might say that a child had more freedom living with him or her than with the victimized parent. Also, the abducting parent "may try to prove that the child lived openly in the abducting parent's home and the victim parent didn't bother to come looking," Michel said. This could show the victimized parent wasn't concerned about how the child was and, therefore, wasn't a good parent. The snatching parent, then, had good cause to take that child.

Michel also questioned a bill that would make the FBI check each custody order to make sure it was valid before starting to investigate. There could be conflicts if there was more than one custody order. Which one should the FBI enforce? he asked.

"Prosecutions would require a victim-child to testify against a parent and thereby exacerbate the emotional trauma for all parties in these cases," he said.

"This, of course, comes on top of the danger to the child that would come with criminalization.

He also pointed out that FBI agents and United States attorneys are already overworked. The bill would place a "severe strain" on their resources. "Investigations and prosecutions would divert precious resources from other areas, such as white-collar crime, public corruption, and organized crime, which have traditionally been the focus of federal law enforcement efforts."

Lee Colwell, executive assistant director of the FBI, also spoke against the bill. Colwell said he shared "concern over the current chaotic situation in which child custody can be litigated again and again, and in which parents with custody rights are left to their own devices in attempting to locate their absconding ex-spouses and their children. The hard work of many able people in developing this legislation is evident," Colwell said.

But he *still* opposed it, and agreed with Michel that the civil part of the bill should be given a chance to work. "Criminalization may increase the potential for violent confrontation and emotional trauma, if not physical danger to the child," he said.

"We believe the threat of arrest is more likely to produce violent and perhaps armed resistance than is a civil recovery proceeding," Colwell said. "Even where no resistance occurs, the sight of a father or mother being handcuffed, frisked, and led away by a number of FBI agents may cause severe and lasting emotional trauma to the child."

He said he thought the bill would force federal criminal courts to decide issues that two different states may already be deciding in *civil* cases. Colwell agreed with Michel that federal investigators and prosecutors would have to determine if state court orders were valid, and would have to decide about how to define *restraint* and *concealment*.

In short, the FBI would have to see if a particular state

court acted properly in deciding custody and visitation before the federal authorities could try a case.

Colwell also said it would be expensive for FBI agents to find children. "A substantial number of additional agents will be needed to handle these misdemeanor violations," he said. "The precise number of additional agent work-years is difficult to calculate.

"If, for instance, the American Bar Association's estimate of one hundred thousand [cases of child stealing] per annum is reasonably accurate, then even assuming optimistically that ninety-five percent of the cases will be deterred or resolved by civil proceedings or by the Parent Locator Service, the FBI would be faced with five thousand kidnapping cases each year.

"Presumably the easier cases will have been resolved, leaving the FBI with the five thousand most difficult investigations.

"Our experience in fugitive-type investigations leads us to expect that approximately one hundred sixty additional agents would be needed to investigate five thousand parental kidnapping matters," he said.

Colwell pointed out that the FBI would also need extra supervisors and support people, and that its efforts to fight foreign counterintelligence and organized crime, plus investigate bank robberies, property crimes, and fugitive investigations, could be weakened if agents had to look for children.

"We question whether it is perhaps anomalous for the FBI to withdraw from investigations of bank robberies and escaped federal prisoners, and at the same time assume responsibility for a misdemeanor involving essentially a family relations problem."

Colwell urged the subcommittee to give those civil portions of the bill a chance to work, and again urged its members to explore other civil areas before "interjecting the federal criminal law enforcement apparatus into these situations."

Louis B. Hays, deputy director of the Office of Child Support Enforcement, spoke for his department against the bill.

"We believe that requiring child support agencies to assume additional responsibilities and caseload would disrupt the administration of the child support program and prevent if from reaching its full potential," Hays said. He also opposed the bill because it didn't make state agencies find children and didn't allow them to charge a fee to find children.

"Further, consideration should be given to financing the costs that would be incurred if the FPLS is made available," Hays said.

The Federal Parent Locator Service might not find children, either, he suggested. "The main sources of home and employer addresses available to the FPLS are records of the Social Security Administration and the Internal Revenue Service," he said. "Both these agencies now have annual reporting requirements. SSA expects to complete recording changes of address contained in the employers' wage reports covering 1978 by April 1980. The IRS records are updated by the September following the April personal income tax filing deadline every year.

"An immediate request to FPLS for location of a recently kidnapped child or the individual believed to have taken the child might, therefore, prove unfruitful," he said.

There were several men at the hearing who represented fathers' rights groups that supported making child stealing a federal crime. Another fathers' rights leader, however, spoke *against* the bills because he felt parents might have to steal children in order to prevent child abuse.

George Doppler gave two examples of incidents where a father might have been justified in stealing his own child, even if he violated a custody order.

"A four-year-old boy was held over an open, lit gas jet by his mother, burning off his nose, his eyes so badly burned the lids were gone, his mouth burned to a continuously open position, his whole face a solid mass of scar tissue," Doppler said.

"A doctor the father took the boy to said he didn't see how the child had kept from breathing so long, for had he, the heat would have burned his lungs and killed him.

"The judge still awarded custody to the mother," Doppler said, along with the other children.

He gave another illustration, of a boy who had broken teeth that were infected, malnutrition, and what appeared to be physical injury to his sex organs. "It was proven that the mother had allowed access of the boy to a homosexual. The mother filed suit for custody and it was awarded to her. The father refused to turn over his son, so the judge placed the father in jail.

"If you were the father, what would you have done?" Doppler asked the committee people.

The Senate passed S.105 as an amendment to the Domestic Violence Prevention and Services Act in June 1980. But the House of Representatives, in passing the act in September 1980, didn't pass H.R.1290, the companion amendment.

Staff members of both houses held a conference and worked out a compromise on the Domestic Violence Act, which included the civil parts of S.105 and H.R.1290, but not the criminal sections. They agreed that all states should adopt uniform custody and that the Federal Parent Locator Service should look for children stolen in violation of a custody order.

They did not make child stealing a federal crime, however, and did not establish any new guidelines for the FBI to look for stolen children. They simply directed the Justice Department to use the Fugitive Felon Act more often in cases where states had issued felony warrants for alleged child abductors. So in order to involve the FBI you still need to obtain: a felony warrant, proof that the child has been taken out of state, proof that the child is in danger, and the cooperation of the home state in extraditing the abducting parent.

In early October 1980 the House of Representatives passed the Domestic Violence Act again with the civil compromises from the parental-kidnapping bills. However, the Act was not brought before the full Senate because of conservative opposition to some of its financial appropriations.

Senator Wallop then attached his parental kidnapping amendment to a bill providing more Medicare funds for the elderly. Both this health-care bill, which had passed the House already, and its new amendment passed the Senate in mid-December 1980.

Those two civil portions of S.105 and H.R.1290, requiring states to honor custody orders from other states and requiring the Federal Parent Locator Service to look for stolen children, became law when President Carter signed the health bill in late December 1980.

However, the anti-child-stealing provisions are not retroactive, and child stealing itself is *still* not a federal crime.

20

Parents' Groups

There is help—and hope.

It comes in the form of parents' groups and information exchanges designed to give advice and support to victims of child stealing. There are only two groups now, but the idea is catching on, growing, spreading from the West Coast to other states, as far east as Ohio, as far south as the Carolinas and Florida.

One such group is the Stolen Children Information Exchange. It helps parents find their children, for free. Two sisters started it after one of their relatives lost a daughter through child stealing. They work out of their homes in Huntington Beach, California.

"While we called around to see how we could help her," said Laurie Cancellara, thirty-three, one of the group's founders, "we saw other people had the same problem. We got to know some of the assistant district attorneys, and one of them said we should take our information and help others. There was no place for parents to go."

Laurie Cancellara and her sister, Barbara Freeman, thirty, run a daily hotline, where parents can call for advice. They have separate homes, but the same telephone number, and work in shifts. One sister will stay home half a day while the other goes out. They take turns counseling parents from all over the country.

Child stealing isn't new to these sisters. Their mother had been stolen twice when *she* was a child. "It was once by each parent," Laurie said, "when she was really small, not more than two years old, and again when she was five or six. She was stolen by her mother, who said her father was a brute. Then, after they'd gotten back together, they had trouble with their marriage and broke up. Her father then stole her to get back into the marriage. It's not a new problem."

After the sisters went on a local television talk show in Orange County, their telephones began to ring. There were newspaper articles and other television shows. In eight months about two hundred parents called.

"The first time we went on television a couple of people who were in California looking for their children called us," Laurie said. "One man in Illinois had given up. We gave him a few tips and the next day he went home with his kids."

Barbara and Laurie refer people to lawyers and private investigators. They also know people in other states willing to help, a loose network of lay people who have lost children and understand the problem.

"Each parent's story is different," Laurie said. "We try to find out if there has been any police contact, because in California we have better laws than in New York." They have learned the law and know what to tell California parents about it.

"Sometimes people don't approach police the right way," she said. "We send them back down and tell them how the law applies and they get out a warrant. We've seen several cases where the custodial parent took the children and the visitation parent managed to get out a warrant."

Sometimes simple advice over the phone can work. "We had one case which was flat out kidnapping," Laurie explained. "The man's name wasn't even on the birth certificate. But the mother called police and said, 'My baby's father took him.' They told her nothing could be done." They went back to the police and got an assault charge on him and he was picked up two days later.

Most of the parents they counsel are women. Of the first 200 cases, there were 160 women who'd lost their children and 40 men who'd been victims. "But with the district attorney's office in Orange County, about forty percent of the children stolen are taken by women," Laurie said.

Part of their help consists of calming down parents. Several parents have come to them so upset and mixed up, they couldn't think of simple things, like checking schools and doctors' offices. "We've had people call us back that day and tell us they had found their kids. They had never thought if school records had been transferred," Laurie said.

Occasionally they get some help from private investigators, who realize how many parents the exchange brings in. "We have detectives who will run little checks for us, like driver's licenses and car license plates. One detective can check traffic tickets and find someone's address that way," Laurie said. "One investigator told several of our parents how they could do it themselves. We also have a good lawyer in Los Angeles who's willing to speak with other lawyers about these kinds of cases."

They're also familiar with the problem of custody orders from other states. "A lot of states don't recognize custody from another state," Laurie said. "They won't cooperate. Arizona is a particularly bad one. So is Texas. Once they get a child there, they take over and do whatever they like. We find the Uniform Child Custody Act isn't enforced."

The exchange does not charge for advice. "We'll never charge a fee," she said. "There has to be *one* place where those grief-stricken people can go. We've had people call and say they had our phone number for two weeks, but just knew if they reached us it would cost money."

They try to help parents find their stolen children and also believe children should see both parents, no matter what, even if it has to be under controlled circumstances.

"Since we've gotten into child stealing," Barbara Freeman said, "I realized that one of my daughter's friends is a stolen child. She told my daughter a different story than she told me. Both stories are different than the one told us by the father.

"Finally, he learned what Laurie and I were up to, because he saw us on the news. His daughter came to my daughter and said, 'If my mommy calls your mommy, don't tell her where we are.'

"I called up the father and told him I wouldn't say where they were, because maybe the woman was as violent as he said she was," Barbara said.

But she checked the district attorney's office for a warrant on the man. There was none, and he had custody. She told him he'd have to take legal steps to keep the mother away, because she probably had a right to visit her daughter. Violating that right by concealing a child can be a felony in California, Barbara told him.

"One of these days she'll get a warrant on him, I said to the father, and then he'd have to fight her from inside a jail and she'd have the child," Barbara said.

"That's the kind of advice we give people. Even if someone *is* violent, you have to do something about it legally," she said.

People ask why she does it, why she and Laurie started the exchange. "Because we can't stand to see so many people getting away with child stealing. Everybody just ignores it and helps it," Barbara Freeman said.

Their address is: The Stolen Children Information Exchange, Post Office Box 465, Anaheim, California 92805. Their phone number is (714) 847-2676.

The Stolen Children Information Exchange is one of only two groups in the country that counsel parents for free. The other is Children's Rights of New York, Inc., which holds bimonthly meetings for parents of stolen children. They also have a list of attorneys, investigators, paralegal counselors, and lay people who counsel parents, which they give out over the phone. They only discuss how-to information about such topics as legal and self-help recoveries at meetings. This group meets in Westbury, on Long Island, and has its headquarters in Stony Brook, New York.

Their meetings provide emotional support as well as paralegal and investigative advice. Most parents of stolen children haven't met anyone in the same situation, and the meetings help them cope. They learn about other cases, find out how parents found and recovered their children, exchange names of new attorneys and private investigators, discuss which attorneys and investigators parents should stay away from. They advise each other about how important it is to keep busy, to not stay home, to never give up. They exchange phone numbers and make friends. Parents who've just recovered their children tell how they did it and talk about how laws and law enforcement authorities in different states helped or did not help them.

Officials from bar associations, private investigators, police officers, assistant district attorneys, and vigilantes have addressed the meetings about various legal, extralegal, and investigative aspects of the problem. Meetings last long into the night sometimes, and parents come hundreds of miles to attend.

Leaders of the group give the latest information on pending federal and New York State bills to help stop the problem. They tell parents which politicians favor and oppose those bills and make copies of them available.

Like the group in California, this organization started because of publicity. There was an article about child stealing in *Newsday* in March 1977, then there were several stories in other newspapers. Victimized parents began to call those parents mentioned in the articles and they decided to meet in the spring of 1977.

By April 1980, there were 407 parents who'd called or

written to this group. Of these, 264 were women who'd lost children and 143 were men. About 300 of these parents have recovered their sons and daughters, some through the courts, but most by themselves. Some hired investigators, some just took friends, a few went with vigilantes.

Not all of those four hundred or so parents had lost their children permanently. With a few, there was only the temporary threat. These cases became custody battles after the absconding parent came out of hiding. But in nearly all of the cases parents fled New York at one time or another.

Their address is: Children's Rights of New York, Inc., 19 Maple Avenue, Stony Brook, New York 11790. Their phone number is (516) 751–7840.

Children's Rights of New York, Inc., is an affiliate of The American Society for the Prevention of Cruelty to Children, a national organization involved in child protection and the enforcement of laws relating to or affecting children. Based in Princeton, New Jersey, the ASPCC has chapters and affiliates in ten states, including Connecticut, New Jersey, Delaware, New York, Pennsylvania (Philadelphia), Kentucky, Florida (Fort Myers), Minnesota (Minneapolis-St. Paul), Texas (Houston), and California (Los Angeles).

There have been other groups that allege to help parents, but most of them have been motivated more by self-interest than generosity. Several victimized parents started groups in order to gain publicity, hoping they might find their children if newspapers and magazines ran their stories. Some succeeded. Others just wanted donations from parents of stolen children in order to lobby, but haven't set up a strong lobbying effort and aren't active.

A number of lawyers have started groups to attract clients. Both the California and New York groups have had lawyers who tried to use their names to build their practices. Child snatching is expensive, and lawyers make most of the money.

Marketing executives and salespeople have set up groups that mail newsletters with pictures of stolen children to schools around the country, police departments, highway patrols, pediatricians. It can be expensive to advertise in them, though, and there is no guarantee you'll learn anything. They charge around six hundred dollars to list a child in their publications.

None of these kinds of groups, set up by lawyers, victimized parents, or mail-order specialists, holds meetings or counsels parents. The lawyers charge for advice and have no referral lists of *other* lawyers, investigators, and lay people, other than their own clients. And neither the victimized parents nor the business people who draft the newsletters will offer any advice. These are business services, not charitable organizations.

Because of its daily hotline, the Stolen Children Information Exchange can reach parents in any part of the country every day. The group has trained volunteers who will counsel people and keeps adding to its list of interested and helpful parents in other states. Working at it full time, sisters Barbara Freeman and Laurie Cancellara devote more time and effort than anyone else to helping parents of stolen children.

The group on Long Island refers parents to the Huntington Beach, California, phone number. Both groups keep in touch each week. "Hopefully, more parents will come forward to help out and assist," Laurie Cancellara said. They already work with custody investigators in many counties in California, and even advise assistant district attorneys about how to handle child thefts.

Most of all, she pointed out, they're making the public and governmental officials aware of the problem, and through their publicity are helping more parents. "We're showing victim parents there is a way out, a solution," Barbara Freeman said. "And the more people we help, the more help *we* get. It's growing and warm, and we keep helping people find their children. Things are far from hopeless. About seventy-five percent of the parents who come to us find and recover their children."

21

Prevention and Legal Response

The best way to stop child stealing is to prevent it before it happens. Know what kind of a parent your spouse is. There are different kinds of child stealers with different personalities. There are those whose behavior is erratic, unstable, who may have emotional problems, an uneven temper. These people move a lot, change jobs, are impatient, angry, have little self-confidence, live in a fury—at society, the world, their boss, their family, you.

They'll move on a moment's notice, quit their job in a fit, think nothing of driving across country on a whim. What they need is therapy and a vacation. What they do, instead, is take their children and drive for days, hoping to leave their problems behind, going it alone where grass is greener, work easier and better paying, and there is no one to question or contradict them. They want to exchange one life for another—leave a cramped apartment or house for a mansion, rent-free, a new start without *you*, but with your *children*. They seek sunshine, clean air, mountains, parks, running streams, peace.

They never find them.

Is your spouse or partner like this?

If parents show little concern for their children, they

might think nothing of stealing them, taking them away from everything they know.

Does your mate help raise your children? Night feedings? Changing diapers? Spoon feedings? Toilet training? It takes *two* parents to bring up children. Can he or she balance love and discipline?

If you are a mother, how does your husband treat the little ones? And you? Would he watch them if you wanted a night off? If both of you work, does your husband help at home? If only *he* works, does he *still* help, especially on weekends? Shopping? Cleaning? (It's *his* home, too.) Is he liberated? Would he be angry if you made more money than he? A man who feels his wife should stay home as a slave is more likely to steal children than one who believes in equal rights for women.

If you are a father, is your wife spiteful? Does she nag? Does she complain? Does she blame all her troubles on *you*? (The same for mothers: Does your husband blame his problems on you?)

Is your spouse violent? A man who beats his wife might steal their children, too. Laurie Cancellara and Barbara Freeman of the Stolen Children Information Exchange found that ninety of the first one hundred women who called them said that their husbands had beaten them before taking their children. Wives can be violent, too. Does your wife throw things?

Has your husband or wife threatened to steal your children? One parent may do so to keep the other in line. If that's the case, you're being given a clue. You're *also* being given time to get ready, to make out your list of what to do if he or she *does* hide.

This kind of person might steal children on an impulse, and is likely to go to relatives or friends. So, if you suspect it might happen, try to stay on speaking terms with your in-laws. Send cards on holidays and birthdays. Mail them pictures of your children. Call once in a while. Besides sounding friendly, this gives you an opportunity to verify their numbers and addresses.

The more erratic and impulsive the person is, the easier he or she is to find. A potential child stealer may just say, "I'll show you," and leave. This happened to several parents on Long Island.

Look for changes in your spouse in his or her attitude toward your children, particularly if he or she never cared for them while married and showed no interest after divorce, and then suddenly wants them. Note if your mate's life has changed as a result of a new marriage, new job, new home, or move to another state. Or if he or she wants your children for the summer after not seeing them for years, something may be about to happen.

Watch out. Many parents have lost children this way. They heard from ex-spouses after many years. Could they put their children on a plane when school was out? They did and never saw them again.

Some child stealers are smarter than others. They are cool, don't tip their hands, have help from family and friends. Though they may drift, be unstable, they know what they are doing when they steal children. They consult lawyers, learn about laws (or lack of them); they take children during normal times, such as a weekend or summer visit; they don't do anything suddenly.

This kind of child stealer often has a predetermined place to go and work once he or she leaves. They have money, and someone to watch the children.

You must think how the parent could earn money if he or she disappeared. Where could your spouse work? Maybe he made a living selling stocks and bonds. But could he *also* be a carpenter? Bartender? Truck driver? Deli clerk? Waiter? Teacher? Secretary?

If the abducting parent is a housewife, does she have

someone to support her? Does she have work, a job which could support her if she left? Relatives or friends to put her up?

How ambitious is your spouse or ex-spouse? Parents who steal children often aren't terribly success-oriented. Parents who *abandon* children often *are*. Always, though, they must earn a living. Most of the time, they take someone with them. The child stealer is not a loner. How could he or she live alone with children in tow? Who would your spouse or ex-spouse be with? It's those girlfriends, boyfriends, baby-sitters who might help you find your children.

If you have any suspicion at all that your spouse might steal your children, make it your business to learn your spouse's social security number and date of birth. Know his or her assets, banks, credit cards, what property he or she owns, where he or she works and lives. Know the same for your in-laws and their friends. Make lists of account and phone numbers and keep them in a safe place along with important papers, such as birth certificates and deeds. Some-times wives go through their husbands' wallets. Husbands can do the same with a wife's handbag. Look for unfamiliar names and phone numbers. Maybe these are for relatives or friends who might help a parent once he or she abducts the children.

If you and your spouse separate or divorce, look for changes in dates and times when he or she wants to see the children. If you have custody, see if your ex-spouse visits them on time. Does he or she pay child support? Does he or she change or cancel visits with the children on short notice? Do the children come home abused? Hungry? Upset?

Always know where your ex-spouse takes them on visits. Some parents pick up children for weekends, say they are going to *their* parents' home, but never tell you where they (the ex-spouses) live. Watch out. Always have a phone number and an address. Say you won't let your children out of the house unless you know exactly where they will be.

If you are an ex-spouse with visitation, make sure your former husband or wife lets you see the children. Make sure there are specific dates and times in the court order that allow you visitation. Does your ex-spouse let you visit? Is he or she fair? Does he or she deny you a weekend with your children? Does he or she make excuses for keeping the kids away from you? (They are sick, busy, out of town, playing with friends, etc.) When one spouse tries to keep children away from the other spouse, it might signal a potential child stealing.

If you can catch your ex-spouse or spouse *before* he or she leaves, but *after* court papers or a travel restriction have been served, you could take him or her to court with a writ of habeas corpus. You should take your children to court and explain you think your children are going to vanish soon and you want to protect their right to see you.

Judges may not give you such a writ and may not put a travel restriction on your ex-husband or ex-wife. They will ask for proof. Has the other parent denied you the children before? Keep a diary. List dates and times *where* and *when* you couldn't see them. Be specific. Try to paint a picture: Your children weren't allowed to see you before, they might be taken away now. Or, if you have custody and think your ex-husband or ex-wife might leave after a weekend visit with the children, keep the same kind of diary. List when he or she failed to visit. Say when he or she changed plans about seeing the children at the last minute.

If possible, bring your in-laws or ex-in-laws to court also. Make them say, under oath, what they know of your spouse's plans. They may be dishonest, but you could take them *back* to court for perjury later.

None of this might prevent a snatch, however. One Sunday night you expect your children to come home and they don't. Or one Sunday morning you expect to pick up your children for a day's visit and can't: They are gone.

Ask neighbors what they know. They probably won't say. But ask anyway. Call your ex-in-laws and their friends. They, too, probably won't say anything. But there's a chance your former spouse took the children there for a short visit and didn't tell you.

If you have a custody or visitation order, call the police the next day. Find out if you can get an arrest warrant on the absconding parent. It might take a few days for police or an assistant district attorney to act. They often want to wait until you are sure your ex-spouse has vanished.

If you have a visitation order, you may have a hard time getting an arrest warrant. Visitation orders are difficult to enforce. Police or district attorneys will say they have more important cases. But, again, try anyway. It depends on the state and county where you live.

If your in-laws or ex-in-laws and their attorney have information about your children's whereabouts, and refuse to tell you, sue them after a month. Bring them into court under writs of habeas corpus. They might not want to be bothered and could turn over your children to avoid such hassles. Make them say they don't know where your children are. You may need proof later that they *did* know, but wouldn't say. In-laws or ex-in-laws and their attorneys often know where abducting parents are and can be accused of helping them.

Sue them for what it will cost to find your children—legal and investigative fees, travel expenses. These suits can start *before* your children come home. Claim they are aiding and abetting your spouse or ex-spouse. What they're doing is unlawful, intentional, and malicious—hiding your children from you. Claim they are causing you mental anguish and loss of affection. They are making you worry and are denying you the love of your children. They are also denying the children the love and affection of one parent.

A second lawsuit you can initiate is for false imprisonment, and is on the children's behalf. People restraining and concealing them deny them their liberties.

Also, under the Uniform Child Custody Jurisdiction Act, you can sue for necessary and reasonable expenses *after* you've recovered the children.

But don't wait until then. File your lawsuits while your children are gone. Make your in-laws or ex-in-laws hire lawyers, pay fees, go to court.

These are civil lawsuits.

Charges against parents for violating custody or visitation orders can be criminal or civil. Violations of these orders are generally either felonies or misdemeanors, which are criminal offenses. But they *can* be civil matters, liable to the charge of contempt of court.

The legal situation is complicated by the fact that punishment for contempt of court might be civil (a fine) *or* criminal (jail) or both. To ensure that the person doesn't get off the hook, try to get an arrest warrant for violating a court order regarding custody or visitation, plus try to get a contempt of court charge for the same thing. This way, though a person might be found innocent of the *criminal* charge of custodial interference, he or she might still be found guilty of the *civil* charge of contempt.

Keep track of exactly how long your children are gone. Try to build a case for child neglect after they've been taken. Claim that child stealing was one of *many* evils your spouse or ex-spouse committed against your children. He or she hurt them emotionally by not seeing them regularly or by not letting you visit with them regularly.

Use this information in order to get a "no visitation" order when your children come home. This order would mean your spouse or ex-spouse can't see the children unless you agree to it or can only see them in your home, in supervised visitation.

A word of caution. Never threaten lawsuits until you feel

you cannot find your children. If you file them too soon, you could stiffen the resistance of the other side. That's why you should wait at least a month before filing them. Get the criminal warrants as fast as you can, though. A felony warrant could be served on your spouse or ex-spouse out-of-state when he or she is found. This will freeze the situation. You will fly to where the children are and pick them up while the abductor is photographed, fingerprinted, and posting bail. Police will turn over the children to you.

You *must* consider these lawsuits, however, besides doing your own detective work, while your children are gone. The threat of false-imprisonment or no-visitation lawsuits *could* make your ex-spouse or spouse and your in-laws or ex-in-laws return your children. And it will keep you active, give you something to do.

22

How to Find Your Children on Your Own

Don't panic if you lose your children. Despite what laws, judges, courts, lawyers, and investigators might or might not say and do, despite conflicts with felony warrants in one state, misdemeanors in another, and despite states rejecting custody orders from other states—you *can* see your children again.

If you want to search on your own, start right away. But don't burn yourself out. Work steadily; pace yourself. Get out of your home each day, keep your job, stay active. Remember, you're not alone. Call the Stolen Children Information Exchange or Children's Rights of New York. It's worth a long distance call. Then try to figure why your ex-husband or ex-wife took the children. Who would help him or her? How would he or she earn money while hiding?

Answers to these questions can start your search. Next, take out pencil and paper.

Make a list of everyone who knows the abducting parent. List them in order of closeness to the parent. Use a red pen to mark people unfriendly to you, a blue to mark those who might be helpful; you will want to treat each differently. Usually people closest to your ex-spouse will not help. People not as close might be friendly.

Then call everyone. Say you only want to know if your

children are fine. Make it clear that all you want to do is talk, to let your ex-husband or ex-wife know how much he or she means to you. Could those friends or relatives get word through to him or her? Could they call someone who knows where he or she is? Could they give a message to your children?

You are a hostage. So are your children. You have to open a dialogue, get people talking. And you have to play your role. Don't say how full of hate you are, how angry you are, how you want to get even.

In fact, calling is part of getting even. You'll make your contacts feel guilty, especially if they have children of their own. Appeal to them as parents. They *must* understand how you feel. What if it happened to *them*? Could they *please* tell your children you love them? Would they forward a letter? Treat everyone the same in the beginning. Find out who will talk, who is a softliner, who is hard. Calling will put pressure on all of them. They'll call each other. Some may not know what has happened. Now they will.

Hardliners will say they don't know anything. Look for quick denials, hostility in their voices, standard answers. "It's none of our business," "We don't know a thing," "Leave us alone." This could tell you they *know*. Try to keep them talking. They may slip, mention a new name, a different city, a job, anything that might be a clue.

Don't do anything that will force the parent further underground. Don't threaten a lawsuit or say you'll get lawyers, investigators, police, or anyone else after him or her. Make your ex-spouse feel guilty, and say that you are helpless, defeated, heartbroken. You want him or her to become careless. You're a nuisance, nothing else. Yet. And don't threaten serious consequences. One mother got her story in *Newsday*. She said how she hoped to get the FBI involved. She would take the Bureau to court if it didn't look for her ex-husband, who allegedly had written letters with locks of hair from the stolen child, letters that said the woman would never see her child again. Such publicity could drive an abducting parent further underground, put him or her on alert, stiffen resistance. Pretend you're weak, but be strong.

If the parent was acting on impulse, if the abduction wasn't planned, he or she won't survive long on the road. If the children were taken in order to get back in the marriage, great. Tell people on your list you, too, want to stay married, if you aren't already divorced. You'll give up custody and money if your mate wants a divorce. Promise everything, give nothing.

Get an answering machine for your phone, or an answering service. You want to take all calls. If hardliners harass you, you'll know who called. If your children try to reach you, you'll know. If your ex-husband or ex-wife gets in touch, you'll know. Don't forget what you want is contact. Only through contact can you gain information. Don't underestimate the amount of indirect pressure you can exert. Though people who don't know about your ex-spouse might not answer letters or return phone calls, they *will* contact those closer to your spouse. What's going on? Is someone they know a kidnapper? Do they know what people down the street have done? They'll say they don't. But they'll call your former in-laws and say you've called.

This will embarrass your ex-spouse. Whole neighborhoods will talk. News will spread, gossip will develop. Write or call people at his or her job. Speak to the boss. Let everyone know what has happened. You can even take out an ad in a local paper. Print pictures of your children. Stick copies of these ads in everyone's mailbox next to where your ex-in-laws live. Don't keep it a secret. One Idaho father took out billboard and newspaper ads in the town where his children were.

If you can't get information from friends and relatives, you should then move to the next phase. This involves contacting all the institutions that could possibly have up-to-date information on the whereabouts of your ex-spouse.

Make another list. What assets does your ex-spouse have? Credit cards? Charge accounts? Property? Include assets of relatives and friends. Write down every name and account number and store or bank where he or she may have done business. (And keep these for future reference in case you later use a private investigator or lawyer.)

Try the school if your children are old enough. Has there been a request for records sent somewhere? Let them send the records, but give you the address. One Long Island father found his daughter in California that way.

Check your children's doctor. Check local drugstores. Maybe they've been called by your ex-spouse and asked to forward records.

Contact credit card companies or charge accounts. If you know your ex-spouse's account number, act like you're still married. You want to pay off the balance quickly. Your husband or wife is careless with money. If you don't know the number, tell them he or she handles all the bills and is on a business trip. You don't want him or her to go over your credit line. Please send all receipts and an interim statement right away. You want to pay off all debts.

One woman in Albany, New York, traced her ex-husband to Reno, Nevada, that way. She convinced a gasoline company to give *all* receipts they had, said her husband traveled a lot and she wanted to pay up. They sent her gas station receipts from Indiana, Ohio, Nebraska, Wyoming, Idaho, Nevada. There were many in one month from a service station in Reno. She got a map of the city and a list of motels. There were five near the service station. She called early in the morning, Nevada time, when she knew her ex-husband would be asleep. When she found which motel he was staying in, she acted like she was his girlfriend and told the clerk not to wake him up.

She had a felony warrant on her ex-husband for alleged child abuse and told police in Albany where he was, and they mailed it to Reno. Police there arrested him and put the children on a plane for Kennedy Airport.

Even though it might cost money, keep those joint charge cards open. Hope your ex-husband or wife uses them.

Motor vehicle departments can tell if your ex-spouse has sold a car, or if its license plates were turned in. Again, be polite. Your spouse is out of town and there is a problem. He or she was going to buy a new car for business trips or vacations to relatives in another state. Things were hectic before he or she left. They're still on the road. You can't call.

Try the job where your ex-spouse worked. Where did they send the last check? Say he or she is on vacation and you forgot the address. They went to visit relatives and the children need some medicine. Do all this before you take out ads or pressure people in your ex-spouse's family.

Try to get your bank to run a credit check on your ex-spouse. This could show a new loan or charge account in a different city. Before a bank or store gives credit, they ask a credit bureau for that person's financial history. It's that history or report you want. It will show an address for your ex-spouse, where he or she will have statements from loans or charge accounts sent.

Also find out from the bank if there is a mortgage payment due. Say you want to pay it before moving, that your ex-husband or ex-wife owned several homes or pieces of land. If he or she sold property, who bought it? *They* may know where he or she went. If your ex-spouse rented, maybe there was a security deposit refunded. Was it given back in person or sent? *Where* was it sent?

Did your ex-husband or ex-wife have insurance? Has that policy been transferred? Say you are moving out of state and that your spouse (again, pretend you're still married) got a policy in your new hometown. Do they have a company or an agent who is handling the new policy? You're just checking because there are so many last-minute details before moving. Give an address for the abducting parent which you know is false. Have them correct it for you. You'll sound more convincing.

Finding your ex-spouse will be easier if he or she has a boyfriend or girlfriend. Perhaps the new lover has children in school, too, or bank accounts, a home, etc. Use the same methods to find *them*. The new lover will have parents, relatives, friends. Start making lists again with hardliners, softliners, motives, assets, etc.

Also, there might be pension or social security checks mailed each month to your ex-spouse. You'll have to use a ruse to get one of those agencies to say where the check is going. A good private investigator can perform such a ruse, or a friendly banker, or charge account clerk.

Where did the power company send its last bill? Again, you may need a ruse to learn where they mailed it. But they may have a forwarding address.

What about magazine and newspaper subscriptions? Has there been a change of address to where a publication should send copies of its next issues? Again, say you are the spouse of a subscriber and that you are moving. Do they have the correct forwarding address? Give the address of a relative in another state. Say you thought your spouse wanted the publication sent there since it will take you both a while to settle in.

Always act like you know what you are doing. With each of these places, give a phony address and say you want to check if that office, magazine, post office, whatever, has the *correct* forwarding address.

Say you're planning on stopping off with Aunt Sally or Uncle Joe and want your mail and bills sent there until you have a new, permanent address. If Sally or Joe are in Montana, and the office gives you an address in Alabama, just say, "Oh, that's right. My husband [or wife] *did* say he [or she] wanted everything sent right away to our new address. We've just been *so* busy I forgot that we weren't going to use Sally or Joe as a temporary address. Thank you very much."

Another method of tracing people is by doing a garbage check. You might find discarded letters or envelopes with an address which will lead to your children. It is difficult, risky, and often requires a great deal of patience. But it can pay off. Go through garbage of people closest to your ex-spouse, people to whom he or she might write letters. Find out which nights they put out trash. Most people put out garbage at night. Determine which can is theirs.

Drive by their home late at night, the later the better. Find out when they sleep. Watch for lights to be out. Bring a garbage can that looks like theirs. Put it where theirs was and take their trash to a safe place. Spread the garbage out and look through it. Piece together letters, envelopes, package wrappings. Then put it all back in their can, return it, and bring your can home. Be sure you leave their driveway the way you found it. This way the collector will find their can full.

Another method is to find out which company picks up their trash. Pay them to put these people's garbage in a separate bag or can and give it to you later that day.

This can work if they use plastic bags for their trash. If they don't and just pour it loosely into cans, they will make it hard, but not impossible, to search. Give that garbage company an extra can or two in which to pour their trash.

"Trash watching" is how Bill Ralston found his children, and how a Long Island mother found her son. It's also helped federal agents learn what a mobster in Arizona was up to. Just hope these people write your ex-spouse, and that he or she writes back. Hope, also, they sleep well, or don't see garbage collectors pour their stuff into separate cans the next morning.

Most people are careless about garbage. They treat it like

what it is—junk, refuse, trash, rubbish. Once they throw something away, they forget it. Hope they throw away a lot.

The best time to trash watch is around holidays, birthdays, Christmas, anniversaries, and other special occasions.

The easiest way to find abducting parents is through phone bills, but it can be dangerous and illegal to obtain them. How do you *get* those bills? *Steal* them. A good private investigator should know, and pay, people in the phone company to read him out-of-state numbers called from those friends or relatives closest to your ex-spouse. But investigators cost money. Suppose you can't find a good one? Or can't afford one?

Stealing mail can be dangerous. You're breaking a federal law. But many people feel the risk is worth it.

What to do is simple. Learn when phone bills go out, when mailmen deliver them. Call a local post office and ask when they deliver mail in certain areas. Again, say you're moving. Call the phone company, too. Give the same story. When do they mail bills? Tell them you're calling power companies, banks, other bills collectors, and want to figure your budget.

The easiest mailboxes to search are in suburban or rural neighborhoods, where boxes are at the end of long driveways and houses are set back from the road. You have to know both when they deliver mail and when the person you're watching is not home. When you think no one is looking, go to the box you want and take letters and the phone bill (but leave magazines so they'll find something). Steam the mail open over boiling water. Don't tear envelopes. Look at their phone bill; write down long-distance numbers. Check the return addresses on any other letters. Steam *them* open, too.

Reseal all envelopes with glue. If you're brave, replace

them in the mailbox. Otherwise, put the mail in a local mailbox. It'll be delivered again the next day.

Some people put mail in their boxes at night for pickup the next morning. You might check their mailbox at night to see if there are any letters to your ex-husband or ex-wife.

Checking mail seems frightening. But how many times has a letter for your neighbor been put in your box by mistake? And how many times have you just walked down the street and put it in that neighbor's box? Or, how many times have you found no mail, then checked your neighbor's box to see if the postman has come yet?

It might be *that* easy. But, remember, you're a stranger. Or, people might suspect that heartbroken parent who called about stolen children several weeks or months ago. It's safer to go by once a month.

What about mailboxes next to front doors? You'd have to search them when no one is home, and you'd have to pick the right day and time.

What about mailboxes in apartment buildings? The only way to get into *them* is to break in. Some people have bribed building superintendents. They often have a master key that opens a whole bank of mailboxes. You don't need to take any mail. You just want to see return addresses. It may work.

What you really need is to get into the home of the parents or friends of your ex-spouse and search it. Parents have done this, some more than once. Several vigilantes claim they've done thirty or forty "black bag" jobs, and demand handsome fees for it. They know what the laws are, know they could face jail. That's why they make the parent pay several thousand dollars in advance, plus put up five thousand dollars for an attorney, if one is needed.

Generally, there is a signed contract. The parent gets back the legal fees if no one is caught. Most vigilantes insist that the parent go with them. If they are caught, they'll claim the parent as a principal. Vigilantes pose as accomplices only.

One vigilante, Samuel Engstrum, thirty-seven, lives in Bismarck, North Dakota. Engstrum joined a fathers' rights group in the Midwest in 1974, after his ex-wife stole their three-year-old son and went to Kentucky.

He soon grabbed him back by breaking into the home of his former-in-laws, where his son was, and taking the boy out of bed at one o'clock in the morning. "I waited until a rainy night," he said, "when they wouldn't expect me." He'd watched the house for three weeks and waited for two situations to develop: rain, and for his ex-wife and her parents to be out. The night he "struck," as he put it, they were all at a party and just a baby-sitter was there.

Engstrum claimed he cut phone lines to the house and forced open the back door with a crowbar. The baby-sitter was asleep on the couch and he woke her up to say he was taking his son, leaving certified copies of his North Dakota custody papers.

"All they could charge me with was trespassing," he said. "The damage amounted to only around twenty-five or thirty dollars. A broken doorjamb and some splinters, and it wasn't a crime to get my own son.

He decided to help other fathers, for a price. It isn't his only income. With two brothers, he owns a farm. They work it whenever he takes to the road, which is every few months. Fathers reach him through the underground.

"It isn't sensational," Engstrum said. "We're not talking about hijacking furniture, bootlegging cigarettes, pilfering garment shipments at airports. We're not thieves. It's just that parents aren't used to this sort of thing and it scares them. Part of the reason I can charge so much is that fear. I'll admit it. I play it up big, tell them they face life in prison and need to put up those attorneys' fees, and *my* fee, to insure safety. I guarantee them we won't get caught, which is impossible. But they don't know that."

Engstrum has his client hire local investigators to watch the home he wants to enter. This could take months. "We want a whole life pattern. We need to know when they entertain, for instance, when they vacation. We might wait six months or so before going in. I was lucky on my own case because I knew my son was there. But in these cases, children *aren't* there. A father coming to recover his son is one thing. Two strangers breaking and entering can be something else. That's why the parent must go with me. We'll have a sympathetic story. Most cops are men and they understand what a guy can go through with his kids and divorce."

Engstrum told what he does, gave a list of questions he wants answered before attempting a break-in, and described what to do.

"When do your ex-in-laws vacation? I always ask," he said. "If you call enough, you might find if they're going away. They could say, 'We don't know where the children are and we're going on a trip so you won't bother us.' "

Good for them, and you, Engstrum explained.

"The best time to get into their home is just before sunrise in the summer. They might have police check once or twice a night while they're away. Neighbors or friends could stop by during the day, see if locks are secure, no windows broken," he said.

Call before you go in, he pointed out. "You *think* they're away. Perhaps they're not. Perhaps someone will house-sit. If a person answers, hang up, control your anger. There'll be other chances. But you call next time and no one answers. Let it ring fifteen or twenty times."

Remember, you're an amateur, he explained. "Overplan. Practice on your own home. Go through the search ten times in your head, five times in your own home or apartment. Draw maps of the house. Hopefully, you've been inside *sometime* while you were married and know where the people keep desks, letters, bills."

Engstrum went into detail about what to look for. "Go to the desk where they keep bills," he said. "Look for bank statements, go through canceled checks. Take any checks you think could prove they know where your ex-spouse is. Most people look through bank statements when they come in and file them. They note each canceled check and compare it to their register or booklet of check stubs in order to balance their account. After that, they usually put away the entire envelope and won't look at it again. If they did, and found a check missing, they'd think *they* lost it, not that *you* had stolen it. Remember, you don't want them to know you've been in; don't leave any traces behind you. Just take what you need.

"And you need the phone bills. As with bank statements, many people will check them once a month and then file them. They won't be missed. Also, look for letters from your ex-spouse or any relative. Some people don't keep letters. You may have been able to pick one out of their trash. Others are neat, however, and keep all letters in a certain place, usually a desk drawer.

"Go through each drawer. Don't tear through the house. This isn't Hollywood. This is your children. You're not searching for drugs or cash, just evidence on where your ex-spouse is.

"Take papers and put them in neat piles on the floor. Bank statements, phone bills, letters, credit card statements, all of these you replace *exactly* where you found them, and in the same drawer, especially.

"What else? An address book, a personal telephone directory, a diary. Address books often are on top of desks. Try to find one. It may have a new listing for your ex-spouse. Also, look for income tax forms. Take these, too. They could prove your former in-laws have money. If you can prove they know where your children are, you can sue them. They willfully, knowingly, and with malice withheld information about your stolen children. Their silence caused you legal and investigative fees and made you suffer emotionally. People look at tax records once a year. Often, they keep each year's copy in order to help fill out *next* year's return. Take them all. They won't miss them, and if they do, they'll think *they* lost them, like canceled checks and phone bills.

"Look at other financial records. Don't steal stocks or bonds or bank books. Just copy down account numbers and balances, how many shares they have, who is the broker. Some people will have investment funds and there might be quarterly statements. These you can take. What you steal is worthless to them, valuable to you. Letters from banks or brokers or realtors you can take also. Again, they're worthless in themselves. But they can show your former in-laws have money. You might sue them for some of this money later, claiming they kept your children from you and should pay your expenses in finding them.

"Go to their phone. Usually next to it will be lists of often-used numbers. Find your ex-spouse's name. There should be a new number. Don't take this list. They use it every day. Copy names of *all* relatives, their addresses, their phone numbers. *They* may know where your children are.

"Look quickly in the phone directory. See if some pages are used more than others. Sometimes people will fold over a corner of a page and underline certain numbers. They might be schools, doctors, clinics, businesses, whatever. See if there are handwritten notes in the Yellow Pages or on other pages. Just thumb through the book.

"What to look for next depends on how much you know about the people. Where would they keep photos? Would they keep letters from your ex-spouse somewhere else? Use them as bookmarks? Put them in kitchen drawers? Before you came in you should have thought all of this out. You have to know what kind of people they are.

"Make a last check of the telephone area and desk. Look for bills or receipts, monthly Master Charge, Visa, Bankamericard statements. See if those cards were used out of state. With department stores, see if they were used to buy clothes for children. If it is your former in-laws' house, your ex-mother-in-law may have bought clothes for your kids and mailed them to your ex-spouse. Take this charge card bill. She could be hauled into court later and asked why she bought baby clothes in June when the children were stolen in January and she said she didn't know where they were.

"What *else* could you find? *Where* could you find it? You should have a list of what to look for. Check it. You might not have another chance. Go to a family room where there might be another phone. Look around it, anywhere you think they might have information on your ex-spouse. Bedrooms, the basement, in an attic trunk? Is there mail from your ex-spouse? Greeting cards? Postcards? Snapshots, souvenirs?

"Before you leave, double-check to see that everything is how you found it," Engstrum said.

If you have no leads, you might have to hire a private investigator, who should have a license to work in your state. They may help find abducting parents who have changed their names or gone into deep hiding.

The first clue that someone has a new name is when he or she cancels credit cards. The person will write to a bank or oil company and say that he or she wants to turn in the cards, close all accounts. An investigator or ex-spouse who checks with those companies and finds cards turned in knows that person is underground.

Try to see those cancellation letters. From where were they written? Did they give a home address? Are former in-laws now making calls to a new city? On holidays are mail watches and trash watches turning up envelopes with a new name on the return address?

Getting information can be easy with a good investigator. How do you find one? Don't hire one over the phone. Ask questions and try to hire anyone on a pay-as-you-go basis.

Find out what they can do. Give them a little time and see what they come up with.

Can they get unlisted phone numbers? Phone bills? Utility bills? Run credit checks? They should work from their offices. Don't have them going around asking questions of former landlords and neighbors. This alerts your ex-spouse you are coming. Landlords and friends probably will protect the parent. Also, you can question people yourself. Remember your lists?

You need an investigator in the town where your ex-spouse lived. This means you might have to hire a second investigator. He could contact banks and businesses there about forwarding addresses. See if the investigator has a list of people like him or her in other states.

Private investigators should have a license from states in which they work. Check to see they do. If they don't, stay clear. There is no way to file a complaint against them if they aren't licensed. Usually the Department of State handles licensing of investigators. That is where you should go if you have questions about someone you've hired.

Find a divorced fathers' group or a feminist group and ask their advice. Lawyers usually have an investigator they work with, but sometimes it's just one. Write down questions. Be specific when you interview an investigator or lawyer. Take your lists of relatives and assets. What can an investigator do with them? And for how much and how long?

A lot of investigators are cowboys—cocky and brash. They boast about playing spy. One said it was fun to watch houses and told how he would use walkie-talkies, have flashlight signals or bird signals, like Indians sneaking up on John Wayne.

An investigator should be bonded and incorporated. Watch out for private investigators who work out of lawyers' offices. All they need is a letter from that lawyer saying they've been hired by him to perform investigative work.

Stay away from one-man, one-room operators working out of run-down offices. They might not have a license or be bonded. Like attorneys, investigators often want thousands of dollars down. And, also like attorneys, they won't tell you exactly what they'll do.

"Just give me two thousand dollars, lady, and I'll find your husband and children," they say.

"How?" you should ask.

"There are ways. I have connections."

Don't give him a dime.

Call or write the Department of State where you live. Ask for a list of licensed private investigators and a set of guidelines they must follow.

23

How to Recover Your Children on Your Own

Once you've located your children, try to get the law to help. Take your custody order to the new state, ask court clerks to register it. You want that new court to recognize and uphold your custody. If it does, you can get a writ of habeas corpus with a writ of attachment. The sheriff can take these to where your children are and pick them up. You, your ex-spouse, and the children will go into court for a judge to decide who should have custody. Or, you might be able to have the sheriff get your children and let you return with them.

Using the law is tricky, however.

First, find a lawyer. Shop around. Go to women's centers or women's groups, or fathers' rights groups. See if they have a referral list. One advantage of these groups is that often, for a small membership fee, you can attend meetings where others with similar problems give advice.

Never go to just one lawyer, and don't hire an attorney who says he or she is the counsel for a certain group. Always ask for lists, and always speak with other lay people in an organization. Some lawyers may hold themselves out as *the* lawyer for a group, but they might do that only to attract business.

Write down questions before you go, just as with investigators. Be specific. Make them say how much they will charge, and what they'll do for you. Then check with other lay people and lawyers. Get a second legal opinion *before* you hire someone, even while your case goes on.

You take a chance by going into court in a second state, though. The judge there might not uphold your custody. He or she might take jurisdiction and decide there should be a new trial. Ask several attorneys in that new state what to do. Be certain you have a chance in court before committing yourself to that method.

If the odds aren't in your favor, you may have to recover your children yourself. You will have to watch the house where your children live, or observe the schools they attend, and wait for the right moment to steal them back. Most parents agree this form of back-snatching or self-help recovering is the only way. It's what keeps John Raleigh and Gene Austin in business. If you do this you will be able to return with them to your home state, where you have legitimate custody.

Recovering children doesn't hurt them, unless there is a fight. That's why timing is so important. Take them when your ex-spouse would least expect it. The best time is when they are going to and from school. The next best time is while they are visiting a friend, if they're allowed out on their own. Avoid crowds and commotion, but try to take them while they're outside on a street or playground.

Waiting for the right moment is hard. You might need someone else to study where they live or attend school. You need to know the routine of both your stolen children and your ex-spouse, or whoever watches and raises them. It could take days or weeks to establish their pattern. Vacations are bad times to recover children because their routines are different then. Holidays are even worse: You could run into your ex-in-laws coming over for a family dinner and reunion.

Once you have that routine down, plan your escape. You

might switch cars, drive side roads, take the least obvious way out of the area. Get maps; check airports, train and bus schedules, rent-a-car offices.

Recovering your children will startle them at first. They may have been told you were dead, or that you hate them, went away, or would hurt them if you ever saw them. They may even run. Plan for the worst. Take things that belonged to them at your home—pictures, toys, favorite clothes. Don't just pick them up from behind and throw them into the back seat, locking all doors and speeding off with you and your children on the floor while a person who is a stranger to them drives. Talk with them. Say you've come to take them home. Explain how you love and miss them, how they'll be safer with you. Say they'll be able to speak with their other parent over the phone, send and receive mail, visit with him or her sometimes, once you're home.

If your spouse abducted your children before a hearing, there will be no custody order in your home state. He or she may have tried to get custody in that new state. It's easy and has been done. The absconding parent gets a new address, says he or she has lived there for at least six months and that *you* have abandoned the marriage. This parent will file for an uncontested divorce. His or her attorney will have the court post a notice in a local paper stating that a hearing on your divorce and on custody of your children is coming up.

You don't see this notice, of course, because you may be thousands of miles away trying to find your spouse and figuring out what went wrong.

Your spouse could then win an uncontested divorce because you didn't know about it.

Check if the parent has filed for custody in the new state. See if he or she has been granted it. Have an attorney or private investigator check with courts in the county where you think your children are. If your ex-spouse does have custody there, he or she can get a felony or misdemeanor warrant on *you* for trying to take back your children.

If there is a custody order giving your ex-spouse the children, you could have trouble overturning it. You'd have to find out what your state, the home state from where your children were stolen, would do with the other state's order. Would they recognize it? If you came home with your children, would your own municipal police, sheriff, or district attorney come after you to enforce that out-of-state order?

This might depend on how long the children were gone, and on how long the new state's custody order has been in effect. If your ex-spouse has custody in the new state, you'd be considered an out-of-state resident asking that custody be given to *you*, an outsider. The judge would have to rule that your ex-spouse obtained an illegal divorce. You'd have to hire a lawyer, prove your ex-spouse is really a resident of another state, the one where you'd lived together. That might not work because of the six-month residency rule. The judge could still say he or she doesn't care if the abducting parent and children lived in another state for ten years. The parent has been with your children in the new state long enough to establish residency.

What can you do?

You could take back the children and immediately go into court at home and claim that all of you are legal residents of your home state, even though your ex-spouse and children have spent those six months somewhere else. You could claim your ex-spouse took the children just to deny you due process. Judges in your home state might support you.

It's the only chance you have and will cost a lot of money in lawyers.

You're at the mercy of the courts again. Your ex-spouse took the children. You couldn't see them. More important, they couldn't see you, and were taken out of familiar surroundings.

Yet here you are, the victim, on the defensive. The burden of proof is on you. You'll have to try and overturn the new state's custody order. You'll have to prove you and your ex-spouse lived in your home state before the separation or divorce, and that you lived there far longer than he or she has lived out of state after the abduction.

The abducting parent would fight, claiming there already is a custody order and no other state should overturn it. He or she will try to prove you and your family lived in that second state, that *you* are the child stealer, that *you* violated the law.

Tom Alexander, head of Male Parents for Equal Rights, Inc., in Wilmington, Delaware, has recovered about forty children in recent years, most of them by using the law. A former sailboat manufacturer, Alexander, forty-one, works full time as executive director of the group. It advocates rights for fathers and gives men divorce counseling.

He works out of a small building, with his office downstairs and apartment, where he lives, upstairs. Divorced, with two teenage children, he estimated he's counseled about 3,600 men since 1975, when he started with the group.

Before he goes out on a case, for which he charges two hundred dollars a day, plus expenses, he researches laws in different states and tries to have county sheriffs help in his recoveries. "I want to know what is required in the new state," he said. "Then I go there and tell them I want to record a custody order from the original state and have a certified copy of it filed in the new state.

"Then I take copies of these papers to the sheriff. Some sheriffs will help. Some want a fee. Some do it for nothing. Some say, 'We can't do anything.' Some say, 'Get me an order from a judge of this county and we'll do it.' And others say, 'There's no way in hell we're going to do it.'

"I simply follow legal procedures for that particular state. I can file a paper in any state in this nation, in any court. When I go to California with a custody order from Delaware, for instance, all I'm doing is recording that Delaware order. Then, if the sheriff is willing to do his job, he'll go with me to pick up the child."

Alexander said that recovering children varies from one section of the country to another. "It depends very much on the individual county," he said. "If you want something done, you want a big county—a county that has a full-time sheriff's staff, no part-timers—and is so big, in fact, that each section operates independently.

"Big urban areas are more cooperative than rural counties. A rural county is most often ruled by the judge. The sheriff, many times, owns the local furniture store and, basically, his people are part-timers.

"In a big city, I don't talk to the sheriff first," Alexander said. "I go to the court first and get my home state's custody order filed, and then go to the sheriff. I ask what his routine is."

Alexander advises parents to stay away from lawyers in the state of an absconding parent. "I've found that every time you get a lawyer involved, you are going to lose in a new state," he said.

"First, the lawyer simply tells you what to do under the Uniform Child Custody Jurisdiction Act. The maximum he can charge is about fifty dollars for consultation. If he decides to take half a day and walks over to the sheriff's office with your duly sealed custody order, that's two hundred dollars. If he says, 'We better file a petition in court to honor this order,' now he can charge five hundred dollars.

"In the state from which the child has been stolen, yes, use a lawyer. Get the custody right. But when you have to enforce that custody in a second state, absolutely not."

He gave an example of a local judge overruling another state's custody order. It was in Florida.

"I'm told there was a custody order from California," Alexander said. "And a second one from New York. Custody was awarded to the father in New York. The mother snatched the kid originally from California to New York. There was a full hearing there and custody was again given to the father. The mother went to Florida. The guy caught up with her and hired an attorney who went into court and asked for the child to be turned over. The judge said, 'Well, I'm going to award custody to the mother.' The attorney said, 'You can't do that, these court orders have to be honored.' The judge said, 'That's true, but as soon as this has been recorded, it will be in the court of Florida, right?'

"The lawyer said, 'Yes.' The judge said, 'All right, go and get it recorded.' The attorney got it recorded and came back. The judge said, 'Now this is a Florida order and under the Uniform Custody Jurisdiction, I can amend the order. It is now amended. Custody to the mother.' That's what happened."

What would *he* have done? "I wouldn't have filed a petition. You don't want to give the absconding parent another hearing, another chance. You're not interested in an argument. You want the kid back in the proper state of jurisdiction. If the absconding parent wanted to contest custody, let him or her come back to the home state," he said.

Alexander said he would have filed the home state's custody order in another county in Florida first, a county where the absconding parent wasn't living. "Then I would have come into the county where the child actually was and attempted to get the sheriff to honor that other county's order."

To recap, there are two steps to recovering your children —finding them, and bringing them home again. The Parent Locator Service might help find your children, but it has no authority to gather them up and hold them in a shelter until you arrive. You'd need those writs of habeas corpus with writs of attachment then. But it still would be up to a judge to decide whether or not to turn over your children to you. But neither the Parent Locator Service nor any kind of writ will help without custody papers.

That's why a criminal warrant is best. It often doesn't help you *find* abductors, but it can bring them in and hold them until victimized parents fly out to recover their children. But sometimes parents are arrested and then let go before police make them turn over the children.

The best approach is to find children, hopefully through the Parent Locator Service, then recover them yourself. Why take a chance in a new state with different judges?

24

Does It
Have to Be This Way?

Child stealing makes some parents desperate. They've spent money on lawyers and investigators, but don't have their children. They have proper court papers, but no one to enforce them. The conflicting laws and the unenforcement of them is overwhelming. Helplessness reduces them to bitter, frantic vigilantes, risking anything for their children. They think of nothing else except seeing them again, and living without them seems to be not living at all, they say.

They try mystics, psychics, tarot cards, black magic; they become superstitious, fearful, paranoid, and have thought so much about why they lost their children they feel they might have deserved it. Are they being punished for being unfit parents? they ask. Only finding and taking back their sons and daughters will make life worthwhile again, they feel.

So they take chances, risk do-it-yourself recoveries and searches without thinking clearly, lose perspective. The following two cases illustrate how tragic child stealing can be.

Jean and Steve Terry, ages twenty-four and twenty-five, respectively, were divorced in Truth or Consequences, New Mexico, in 1976. Steve won custody of their three-year-old son, Bobby.

But Jean stole the boy and gave him to her father, Fred

Sampson, who took him to Tishomingo, Oklahoma, where the Sampsons lived. She stayed behind a few hours to gather clothes before joining her father.

Steve caught her, though, and police arrested her for alleged custodial interference, a felony. The Sampson family tried a deal: If Steve would drop all charges, they would give up his son. Only there was a catch: He'd have to come to Oklahoma to get Bobby.

Steve made a mistake. He agreed to drop those charges *before* recovering his son. With three friends, he left for Tishomingo in a private plane.

While he was gone, Jean pretended she was sick. Police took her to a hospital, where she escaped, called her father, and told him not to turn over her son. Then she left for Oklahoma and got home safely.

Steve Terry went to the Sampsons' house, where Fred Sampson waved a shotgun in his face and told him to leave. He returned to New Mexico with his friends and filed more charges against his ex-wife. One was on the original charge of child stealing. A second was for civil contempt of court, violating a custody order, and a third was for jailbreaking.

Terry again went to Oklahoma and hired an attorney. He tried to get police there to honor his New Mexico custody order and arrest warrants. Oklahoma refused. They granted custody to Jean.

Now there were two orders: one from New Mexico giving young Bobby to his father; a second from Oklahoma giving custody to his mother. Tishomingo police also refused to extradite Jean on the New Mexico criminal charges.

Terry found Gene Austin and John Raleigh, the custody vigilantes. They watched the Sampson ranch.

"Jean's father had a shotgun and her uncle had a pistol strapped to his hip," Raleigh said. "It was like the Old West."

"We spent a solid week laying in the woods with ticks and bugs," Austin said, "trying to figure how to get through that wall of guns. We laid out there right across the street from

Jean's house. It's two houses on a small ranch, about five hundred or six hundred acres, six or seven miles outside of town."

Austin, Terry, Raleigh, and Terry's friends gave up. They went to the governor's office and asked for an investigation. New Mexico wanted Jean for jailbreaking. Why didn't Oklahoma arrest her and send her back? The governor's office promised to look into it.

"Gene went home and the father went home and evidently he got impatient," Raleigh said. "Steve was a young guy and not very patient I gathered from conversations I had with him after that. He and his friends flew to Tishomingo again, rented two cars and parked one of them in front of Jean's house."

They went to her door one hot Friday night in late July, said their car had broken down. Could they use the phone to call a garage?

Jean's sister let them in. They tied her up, took the boy, and ran out.

But they'd made another mistake.

They hadn't watched the house and didn't know that Jean and her uncle were in there.

When they heard what happened, they ran to a pickup truck and chased Steve and Bobby, who were in a rented car. Steve's friends were in another.

Jean's uncle hit the back of Steve's car. Steve wouldn't stop. He wanted to leave Oklahoma, and drove faster and faster.

The uncle bumped him again. Steve speeded up even more.

Then the pickup pulled alongside, tried to pass, and cut him off. Both vehicles sped side by side.

What happened next is unclear. Newspapers and magazines gave different accounts. Jean said one thing, Oklahoma police another, Gene Austin and John Raleigh, who spoke with Terry's friends afterwards, have a third version.

The Oklahoma Highway Patrol said Steve Terry swerved when Jean's uncle tried to pull beside him. The pickup ran into the rear of the car carrying Terry and his son. The car hit an embankment and overturned three times.

Jean said *she* drove the pickup. "I tried to pass them several times," she said. "But their car must have lost control. It flew into a ditch and rolled over twice before smashing into a tree."

John Raleigh told how the pickup rammed Terry's car several times. "When that didn't do the trick, he [the uncle] pulled alongside of him and forced him off the road," Raleigh said. "The car turned over a couple of times and ended in a ditch along the roadside."

Each story has the same ending.

Young Bobby, three years old, died instantly, Steve Terry a day later.

Police arrested Steve's friends and charged them with second-degree murder and kidnapping. The uncle who pursued them was not charged.

The Sampson family went to court and got an order that kept the Terry family from little Bobby's funeral. They buried the child in Tishomingo. Steve's body went back to New Mexico.

Doris Kossman lost her children at about the same time that Steve and Bobby died.

She had two sons, Timothy, six, and Matthew, four. Doris won custody after her divorce. But her husband stole the boys in 1976 and she hadn't seen them or received a telephone call or postcard since.

She felt she couldn't live without her boys. Some nights she would wake up thinking she'd heard them cough. Matthew had trouble breathing and was scheduled to have his adenoids taken out, but his father, Marty, stole him and his brother before doctors could operate.

The boy had colds every winter. He needed medicine,

Sudafed, Actifed, prescription drugs. Was he getting them? She'd wake up at three o'clock in the morning and wonder. She had dreams where she thought her sons were home. Matthew would cry. She'd get up. Timothy would climb down from the top bunk, run to Doris's room. She'd be awake, putting on her nightgown. They'd go to the bathroom, search the medicine cabinet.

It would be empty.

Doris would dress her children. It would be hard with Matthew coughing and crying and Timothy crying because he didn't know how to help his brother. She would drive them to an all-night pharmacy, still in her nightgown. It was always winter, icy roads, threatening weather, gas stations closed.

The pharmacist would say they needed a new prescription. There were no refills on the note she'd left weeks before from their doctor. She would ask for some cough syrup. There would be none.

Her dreams, now nightmares, ended with car trouble.

Then she'd wake up, check the boys' room. It was empty, and she'd feel relieved, at first.

Then she'd realize they were gone. Maybe her vision was true somewhere else. Maybe it was their *father* who drove at night to drugstores. Or maybe he wasn't even home. Timothy might wander to a neighbor's, ask for help, find none, lose his way.

She was afraid for them.

Then one night after one of these nightmares, she took too many sleeping pills. Friends got to her while she was on the phone and took her to a hospital.

It was foolish, she admitted, and people came over, stayed a few days, listened to her fears and anger. Everyone said to get her children.

"I mean *everyone*," she said. "A family court judge, a police detective, my lawyer. They called it 'self-help.'" But she had to find them.

She lived this way for three years. Her nightmares came twice a week.

Doris Kossman had been to several lawyers. They didn't know who to serve with writs of habeas corpus. She told the Parent Locator Service that she still had the children and her husband didn't send child support. They couldn't find him, either. Marty had been a stockbroker, but not anymore. He didn't file income returns or pay social security taxes.

A friend, who was a nurse, and her family doctor tried to help her trace them by calling hospitals and pharmacies in San Francisco and St. Paul that might have treated Matthew's adenoid problem. They checked every three or four months, from July 1976 to June 1979. But they found nothing.

Then she decided to visit her ex-husband's sister and mother. Doris wanted to make the trip by herself, but her girlfriend, Maureen Pey, went with her. She had two weeks' vacation and loaned Doris the plane fare.

They went to Minnesota first, knocked at the sister-in-law's house on a Sunday afternoon. She wouldn't see them. They pleaded. There were packages for Timothy and Matthew. The woman suspected tricks and called the police. The two women left before squad cars pulled up.

Maureen wanted to make it a vacation for Doris, too.

They flew to San Francisco, and checked into a second-class hotel.

"My boys will be in school," Doris said. "Let's check the Board of Education before going to his [her husband's] mother's house." She had certified copies of her custody papers, her sons' birth certificates, her birth certificate and driver's license from New York.

A clerk at the Board of Education didn't believe what they said.

"We had friends on Long Island," Maureen told her, "and they moved to California a year ago. We lost track. Now we're visiting and want to look them up. Their kids and our kids were best friends."

"Did you try the phone book?"

"They always have unlisted numbers."

"School's closed now."

"We know; we thought they might register for the fall."

"I don't know."

Doris saw that the clerk, a woman in her late thirties, wore a wedding ring.

"Do you have children?" she asked.

"What do you mean?" the woman said.

"Well . . ." Doris looked at Maureen and took a breath. "We're looking for my sons. Their father stole them."

"What?"

"Three years ago."

"Why did you come here?"

"We thought . . ."

"What about police, the FBI?"

Doris told her. "Here are the custody papers. Look, you don't have to say we were here."

"But you *are*."

"No one else has talked to us. Only you know who we are."

The woman looked at them. "I guess records *are* public documents."

"He doesn't have to know how we found them," Doris said.

"Wait a minute."

The woman went into another office. She came back with a large notebook.

"What was the name again?"

"Kossman. His mother's name is Bishoff," Doris said. "She remarried. On Geary Boulevard."

The woman looked up. "No Kossman, Timothy or Matthew. What are their middle names?"

"Andrew and William."

She looked again. "None of them, either. I'll check under B."

"Thank you."

The clerk came back with a second large notebook. "Beschkoff, Bishkoff . . . Sorry, not here."

"All right."

Doris and Maureen went to their hotel. "It's useless. My sons aren't here. What do we do? Check the boards of education in every city?"

"Marty likes boats," Maureen said.

"That narrows it to coastal cities and those on rivers."

"Doris, we need a night off. Let me take us to dinner."

"I can't eat."

"We'll try tomorrow, okay? His mother must have their address."

"I don't think so."

Maureen treated them to Ghiardelli Square that afternoon. Fog came in under the Golden Gate Bridge. Sailboats made white triangles on the bay. Sunset shone orange from windows in Berkeley and Marin County.

"All I see is Alcatraz," Doris said.

"Look, it's been a week. We're not having fun."

"I know, Maureen."

They looked at each other. Her friend reached over. "I didn't mean it, Doris."

"And you have another week left. Can you go somewhere else? I'm bad company. This is *my* cross. You've done enough."

"Can't leave you now."

"I want you to. Please."

"You'll be alone. Might do something foolish."

"Not any more foolish than what we're doing now. Ruining your vacation."

"I have relatives in San Diego," Maureen said.

"Good. Check schools for me."

Doris drove her to the airport that evening. It was a quiet

ride. They went along Nineteenth Avenue through Golden Gate Park and then to Lincoln Way and the skyway. There was cracked, gray Kezar Stadium and tall buildings down Oak Street with peeling paint and broken shutters and vacancy signs in red letters. Long-haired hitchhikers stood near the entrance to the skyway.

Sunlight came off the Bank of America building and the TransAmerica pyramid. The Bay Bridge was in front of them, Potrero Hill, with rows of Victorian houses painted red and blue and pink and yellow, on their right. Children played before some of them.

"I wish you'd let me go to his mother's," Maureen said.

"She hasn't told for three years."

"She might if she *sees* you. And *us.*"

"I don't want anyone with me."

"You've been alone before, Doris."

"And I did all right. I'm through that. I'll try the coast, drive to L.A."

"Call when you get there."

"Of course."

"See you in a week. Promise?"

"Let me work off steam, Mt. Carmel, Aptos, Santa Cruz. I have maps."

"You might not find them."

"I've lived with that."

"Good-bye." Maureen hugged her and then got out of the car. "You know where to call."

"And I know what I'm doing. Don't worry."

Doris drove back to her hotel and turned in her rented car.

The manager found her two days later. A chambermaid told him she couldn't get into Room 512 to change the sheets. A Do Not Disturb sign hung on the doorknob. They knocked, but there was no answer. Records showed she hadn't checked out.

He found her fully dressed, hair in place, wearing a black

business suit. Pictures of Timothy and Matthew were in small frames on her night table.

There wasn't a note.

It doesn't have to be like this.

With federal laws that force states to approve each other's custody rulings, with criminal penalties that might prevent child stealing, these kinds of cases might not happen.

There could be more than just new laws, however, more than just the Federal Parent Locator Service to look for children. There could be federal, state, and local agencies, public and private, to counsel parents, offices where parents can turn when they first lose their children.

There could be more human rights for children in divorce, which would mean a change in attitude for governmental officials, courts, judges, lawyers, police. Human life should come before money and property in divorce settlements. Stolen children should come before stolen cars.

It wouldn't be hard. It's not a question of changing the world overnight. The federal and state machinery is there already. The government has an opportunity to find and recover children without spending extra monies. It won't have to form new agencies, buy new equipment, train new personnel, make new studies.

Using the Federal Parent Locator Service to find abducting parents is just the beginning—a step, but not a solution. There must be criminal warrants, threats of jail to prevent parents from stealing their children. There must be an agency like the FBI, which could find and arrest an absconding parent *and* pick up stolen children at the same time.

Parents will still fight and divorce, but they might not steal their children if they knew they'd break a federal law by doing so; if they knew a federal warrant could be served in any state; if they knew they'd be watched every time they cashed a check, made a phone call, charged a meal, got a job.

How many children could be saved?

Appendix

Parental Kidnapping— A State Survey of Laws

States treat child stealing under custodial interference sections of their penal codes. There are three classifications: One, to make it a felony if a child is taken in violation of a custody order no matter *where* that child may be taken, inside or outside the state;

Two, to make it a felony only if the child is taken *outside* the state and to make it a misdemeanor if the child remains *inside* the state;

And, three, to treat it as a misdemeanor only.

States that treat child stealing as a felony no matter where the child is taken are Arizona, California, Colorado, Illinois, Indiana, Massachusetts, Minnesota, Montana, Nebraska, Oklahoma, Virginia, Washington, Wyoming.

States that treat child stealing as a felony *inter*state and as a misdemeanor *intra*state are Alaska, Arkansas, Connecticut, Florida, Georgia, Iowa, Kansas, Louisiana, Maine, Missouri, New Mexico, North Carolina, North Dakota, Ohio, Oregon, South Carolina, Texas, Wisconsin.

States that treat child stealing as a misdemeanor are Alabama, Delaware, Hawaii, Kentucky, Maryland, Nevada, New Jersey, New York, Pennsylvania, South Dakota, Utah.

There are six states which don't have custodial interference statutes. Some have kidnapping laws which may or may *not* apply to child stealing. These are Idaho, Michigan, Mississippi, Rhode Island, Tennessee, Vermont.

The District of Columbia, New Hampshire, West Virginia, and the Virgin Islands have no statutes relating to custodial interference, kidnapping, or related offenses.

Parents or their attorneys should review current state laws before starting legal action. An up-to-date source of information about state, federal, and international laws regarding who has jurisdiction over child custody disputes is The Child Custody Project, American Bar Association, Second Floor South, 1800 M St., N.W., Washington, D.C. 20036.